WICKED DREAMS GOODNIGHT

A WITCHY FAIRYTALE

AMANDA L. BALL

Wicked Dreams Goodnight
a witchy fairytale
Written and published by
Amanda L. Ball

First Edition
Paperback ISBN: 979-8-9922822-3-8
Hardcover ISBN: 979-8-9922822-4-5
eBook ISBN: 979-8-9922822-5-2

For permission requests, please contact the author at:
contact@digitalmedleys.com

* * *

For more content, follow the author's work on social media:
@echoendlessmind

To the women—the friends—who have loved and supported every bit of me, who have witnessed me—weary bones on the outside, passionate soul on the inside, and all of the in between. I hope you know how much you all inspire me every day. I love the colors of your heart.

Misha, Zoë, Mandy, and Alissa—thank you all for being a part of my story and for showing me what friendship means. ♡

To Mom,
You never, ever stopped believing in me. Thank you for being my biggest fan.
I love you,
♡ Amanda

Though we are buried in a misogynistic, patriarchal world,
as women, we must keep pushing through, laughing,
celebrating, uplifting, existing...
because the toxic men cannot fucking stand it.
Keep going, ladies.
If their heads are exploding,
it's working.

We connect through our souls,
and if you quiet your mind
you can feel the good ones.

♡

Table of Contents

Dear Reader,

After releasing my debut poetry book, *Storm of Enchanted Dreams: a poetic fairytale*, in January 2025, I realized that my heart was always in love with fairytales, nursery rhymes, and lullabies. As adults, we deserve those stories too—though in a more relatable fashion. I wanted this second poetry fairytale to be darker, like *Grimms' Fairytales*, with my typical, whimsical Shel Silverstein, Mother Goose, and Dr. Seuss style (my favorites growing up).

I am a feminist woman, author, poet, and I am a loud, relentless voice for women—all women—and other marginalized groups. I do not write to please the masses; I write to connect to an audience that is much like myself. Too often I have been called a "man-hater" because of my feminist views. I do not condone violence, but I will stand strongly beside any woman who has been harmed by a man. The evil, controlling, toxic behavior must end, and women should finally be viewed as the beautiful (and sometimes dark) souls that we are. Writing has always helped me with getting all of those emotions of anger, resentment, and revenge out—my pen is my weapon of choice.

This book is for all the women out there who have had similar thoughts and feelings or who grew up feeling different—the black sheep, if you will (or *Black Rabbits*, as you will read). Your beautiful *Gothic Heart* is safe within these pages. Take care of yourself, but most importantly, take care of one another.

To the men on our side, thank you for seeing us all as women— as human.

Hold on tight for this dark fairytale adventure.

♡ Amanda

The Witches' Tale

Come along for the ride,
let me weave you a tale
of the little goth girls
we all know so well

they always try to hide
out of sight, out of mind,
but their dark clothes,
dark hair, dark eyes
stand out instead
and they can't hide

from the world's stares
and judgements, raining down
in a pool beneath them

and I will tell you how they win...
though, it's a secret—what they
do to them

so, you must promise not to tell,
for this is a story *not* for history;
this is a story from the witches
who come *after* you...

they will honor each one of you
and they will do it well;
the plan is already in motion,
so, come, and hear my tale.

Once Upon a Time...

Once upon a time
in a dark castle atop the hill,
lived a witch who was fed up
with evil men...

One day, she set out
with her black cat,
and black cloak, and
black bag
searching for her coven—
more dark, witchy women—
hoping to make a difference.

Deep in the forest
they gathered,
their familiars all around—
spiders, ravens, crows,
black cats and bats,
owls, and snakes, and rats.

They brewed their potions,
chanted their spells,
threw in a few hexes and
curses.

And all across the land,
the evil ways of man
were no longer a woman's
burden.

This is their tale
that I will tell,
weaving it like a fable;
though, the truth
of it is, that all of
the witches were really
just powerful women.

Quest

Journey to the edge with me,
bare your battle scars.
Slay the dragons in our wake;
victory will be ours.

Challenge our enemies to a duel
and rescue those in need.
Destroy the barricades in our way;
don't be afraid to bleed.

Follow the light in from sea,
climb the tower to the top.
Steady your arrows,
wait in the dark;
we'll stay the path
and never stop.

We know the evil that exists,
we've seen this all before.
We may lose a battle or two,
but we can win the war.

Our nemesis is teaching
their children their ways.
We must break the
cycle now.
There is more to life
than hate and greed.
Let's make our
descendants proud.

The warriors before us
paved us a way.
They dug their graves
and laid down their lives
so we could see a better day.

This combat is about
right versus wrong,
and the innocent are
counting on us.
Let us joust till we collapse,
but triumph is a must.

I know our bodies
are feeling weak,
we've marched and fought
and bled;
but we will not surrender,
we will defeat instead.

If you feel all hope is lost,
or that this crusade feels endless,
remember that monsters
can be vanquished,
that all creatures can
know freedom.

So come along
to the battlefield,
join me on this quest.
If we advance on together,
we can liberate the oppressed.

Death of the Patriarchy

We sit up.
We get up.
We hear all
the words
that say we cannot,
that tell us our worth.

We begin to believe it,
but we are so damn
sick of it,
so we say
enough is enough.

And when we stop allowing,
and we stop cowering,
we are called all the names
in the book.

We are convinced we are
weaker,
we are made to feel meeker,
so that we continue
to be unsure.

But when we are silent
we prepare our weapons,
and we conspire
to wage the war.

We sit up.
We get up.
We notice who
stands by our side,
as we take up arms
ready for this fight.

We slay the dragons
who told us we are weak.
We slay the dragons
who never allowed us to
speak.

We slay the oppressors,
and the second-guessers,
who weren't prepared
for us to fight back.

We call on our sisters
and the men who stand with
us,
we call on all those
who can see

when women are respected
and control is rejected
we can all live
harmoniously.

Until then, we fight,
we take back our right
to walk alone
without fear.

And with these weapons
inside me,
I dare you to try me,
as I am the woman
they warned you about.

The type that says *no*,
that doesn't give you control,
and my army is
always around.

If you're not with us
then you are against us,
and we are coming
for you.

While you were
disrespecting,
we were all plotting
and we will see this
war through.

We slay the dragons
who thought they were coy.
We slay the dragons
we *tried* to avoid.

It is *your* persistence
that finally caused this,
and your ego that has
drawn out my sword.

Keep on with your words,
they provide me more fuel
as I sharpen my weapons
with ease.

For you still cannot see
that your time is near,
and *your* kind are the ones
who are weak.

Feminist Rage

We tried.
We tried to pour love
out into the world,
to smile,
to forgive.

We tried.
We tried to be polite,
to speak when spoken to;
only to be chastised,
groped, belittled...
made to feel fear.

We tried to "go high"
when they went low.
We really
really
tried.

We tried to walk away.
We tried to be nice.
We tried to play fair.
We tried to be quiet.

Though, from the fire
we tried to put out,
the embers of our flame
could not be watered down.

The fire could have been
prevented
had they just left us
alone.
They sparked the fire
of rage in our souls.

And they expect us to remain
silent,
to lay down and die;
they want us to give in,
with no meaning to our lives.

They're building soldiers,
and we don't know who to
trust;
they say they'll let us live
if we can just

lay down our bodies,
do as they please,
if we were to beg
nicely
down on our knees.
But they forgot...
angry women
don't go quietly.

It is in you.
It is in me.
It lived in our ancestors
and it's being set free.

Their soldiers are coming—
march one, two, three;
but warriors march
to a different beat.

We know all their moves;
history repeats.
But they don't know how to
handle
the rage at our feet.

Now is the time
to write a new story,
to burn it down—
the patriarchy.

Pack up your poison,
conceal your daggers,
tuck your scissors
behind your back.

We've always known
when to smile sweetly,
innocently...
when to perform
and when to attack.

They march at dawn,
while we enjoy our tea,
while we sharpen our
knives...
and sharpen our teeth.

If they want us in the
kitchen,
that's where we'll be.
After all, we can make
arsenic
taste quite sweet.

They're getting closer,
they've made some gains,
though they have
underestimated
our feminist rage.

Wicked Dreams Goodnight

The Webs We Weave

The Edge of Darkness

I have walked miles
in every direction,
lost and clueless
as to where I was headed.

Searching through the dark,
my compass malfunctioned,
wishing to find an indication
of where I should be going.

The forest of trees
is getting darker,
the storm's winds and
rain becoming heavier.

My soul is withered,
my heart is torn,
my mind attempting
to hold on

just a little longer
until the storm is through;
my aching bones—
weakening—
are guiding me askew.

I search desperately
for higher ground,
climb to the top of a hill
so I can look around

and hope to find shelter,
a place where I can rest
and clear out all these
demons
stirring in my head.

But the winds are getting
heavier,
the rain blinding my eyes,
tipping over the edge of
darkness...
hoping I'll learn to fly.

We're All Going to Die

You cried when Bambi's
mother died,
and Simba's father,
too.
Sometimes it's hard
to understand why some
leave this life
too soon.

Though, the universe
needs our souls
to power more stars—
to light up the sky;
and it often feels
unfair.

Maybe it's a heaven,
maybe it's a hell;
or maybe our energy
is simply floating
around in the air.

Some may become
an angel, a demon,
or a ghost;
though there is no way
to know for sure
where our souls will go.

The one consistent
certainty in life
is that this planet
is not our eternal
home.

So, darling girl,
dry your eyes,
we all know—
it's no surprise...
eventually,
we're all going to die.

And I promise you this,
life will keep moving,
spinning here on earth's
floor;
don't be afraid of
what's to come;
death is just goodnight.

Becoming

Slipping through the cracks in my bedroom floor,
trying so desperately to reach the door;
the room now spinning,
the lights gone out,
nothing left
but fear
and doubt.

Extending arms searching for something to grasp,
memories flooding like broken glass;
cuts sever the skin deeply
as I try to prevent my soul from weeping;
tears stained on the walls,
my mind racing in a world of dark.

Quicksand pulling,
my feet go numb,
heart is pounding,
my body is done.

Every morsel that I feel
slipping and sliding as I heal,
weighing on me,
pulling me down,
my mind feels even
heavier now.

My pen, my weapon,
finds my fingers
and out spills all
of the pain that lingers.

Swooping and swirling,
I've lost control,
my pen is driving
the words of my soul.

Get it out,
every ounce;
as the ink
leaks
it sheds some
doubt.

And I am coming up for air,
feeling weightless,
my soul has bared
all of its anger,
all of its truth,
hidden inside stories
within pages—
an endless loop.

As I carefully review my work,
I feel it again—
all the angst and the hurt;
though, I can carry it better now;
one becomes stronger after
they almost drown.

Rotting in My Own Prison

Down the winding staircase
in the cold, dark dungeon
locked behind the bronze steel gate,
I battle with my demons.

The guards come in to feed me
and offer me sips to drink,
then I am alone once again,
nothing to do but think.

These chains are getting heavy,
digging deep into my skin,
tethered to the metal furnace
with a draft coming in

through the open window, so small
and so high, I cannot see outside;
I wonder if the moon
is full tonight.

I return to my task,
etching on the wall,
trying so hard to construct
a tunnel I can crawl

through to reach the other side,
why must this torment keep me here—
stuck...alone...dying...
only myself to fear.

Toxic Love

How can I not feel starved
carrying around this empty heart?
Growling at me like a hungry toddler,
screaming bloody murder.

Craving them is like craving
a poisonous apple,
a fall from a bridge,
a bite from a snake.

And still, I am lying here starving.

Give me a fairy godmother
who can take it all back;
a genie in a bottle
who allows three wishes;
I'm not sure what
I did to deserve this.

Give me a wizard's wand,
a witch's spell,
a penny for the wishing well,
anything to allow me to
go back to the beginning.

I could choose a different path,
get my lost heart back on track,
find someone who
would never poison me
the way that they do.

Please, Goddess, give me
another fork in the road,
a decision made by my soul—
not this desperate, dark, black heart;
give me a compass to take me
back to the start.

I would rather journey on my own
and drag around a heart of stone
than live even one more day
with memories of them
filling up this space
inside my head,
inside my bones;
please rid me of this toxic love
that has taken a hold
and latched itself on...
leaving me with
a toxic soul.

Drained Hourglass

I walked across oceans
swam over the bridge
danced on top of shards
buried in dirt

swept out to desert
thirsty at sea

discombobulated
misunderstood
desperate to be free

find my heart
patch up my soul
fill in the gaps, the gaping holes

with stones, and salt,
filled with sand

as it flew in the wind
out of my hands

and I lost it...

Wicked Heart

They play with our hearts,
they play with our scars;
they push us back
until we fall.
We say *no more*,
then we show back up,
telling ourselves,
that's just love.
But love doesn't hurt,
love doesn't harm;
love is being safe
in somebody's arms.
Love isn't hateful,
love isn't dark.
Love is the glue
that binds your
wicked heart.

Battling My Demons

Oh, the demons have come out
to play
though I did not invite them to
my party.
I ask to choose another
day,
but they've already gotten
started
drinking the punch,
making new friends,
talking to people
I don't want them to meet;
and so I run around clumsily,
trying to push them back out
to the street.
But the music is blaring,
and everyone is dancing,
and I just can't get them
to leave.
And so I must learn
to welcome them home,
for they will never
let me be.

My Soul's Existence

It's the unspoken hurt we keep locked up tight,
trying to hide the pain from outside eyes;
smile and wave, *hi*,
concealing all the truth inside.

It is not that we are lying,
we are just desperately trying
to keep the world from seeing us crying—
we don't want that burden on anyone else.

And so, we suffer longer,
hoping we will magically become stronger,
though, we are always longing
for a place of belonging.

Unlike many, I do not see beauty
in my simple existence;
I look for beauty in the world around me—
in the creatures and the friendships.

The world is quite an unkind place,
hate and greed always in our face,
who created this human race...and why?
We were forced here to suffer and die.

Eternity sounds so very peaceful,
but we keep turning more resentful
because religions tell us who
we are supposed to be...
not exactly free.

Like in school,
if we do not follow the rules,
we will have to sit out at recess
when we are meant to be the freest.

And so, we box it all up tight,
lock the truth deep inside,
out of sight from prying eyes,
so that we can control
the direction our soul goes
when it is time to say goodbye.

Heaven and hell?
Who could tell?
I choose freedom over religion,
for I am in control of my soul's existence.

Rebel

To not follow religion is to not follow a crowd, to rebel
against the constant barrage of demands and reminders that your
self
is destined for hell,
that you do not know better than the dictators who
constantly tell
us all we must not know ourselves
very well;
for all those temptations, and all those desires,
and all those opinions will send us to the
fire
if we love who we want, if we take our own path, if we walk
away and
never
look
back
on the family, the religion that calls us
sinners;
forging a new way is just the
beginning;
I never wanted to follow the crowd,
I always intended to be different—stand out;
and so, I was labeled and judged, because
I didn't fit into the box that they made me;
I prefer my coffin, in the dark, red
velvet
casing.

Cave of Turmoil

If only they knew
the depths I had to
crawl
out of my own
dark mind
to emerge
into the light.
In a dark cave
I stumbled into;
how did I even
get there?
A lifetime of angst,
holding it all in,
building it up,
close to combustion;
Goddess, please, don't
let me go
back
there
again.

Lyssa

Falling to my knees,
screaming
into the abyss;
the Goddess of Anger
calls to me.
I heed her call,
unaware of her cause,
up off my knees,
advancing without pause.
She steers me through
the gushing winds,
keeps me on my feet;
I do not ask her motive,
I allow her to move me
in the direction she is
calling to me.
Bolts of lightning
tearing through,
striking branches,
burning roots.
But still I keep going,
she keeps me steady...
until the blinding rain
becomes too heavy—
seeping through my
ice cold clothes,
staining the walls
of my soul.
I really need some
shelter now,
if I don't act quick,
I will surely drown.

Though, the Goddess of
Anger
does as she pleases;
she pauses for no one,
she signed no treaties.
And so, I must
weather this storm,
and hope tomorrow
a kinder Goddess is lured.

"Not All Men"

"I would never..."
"That's not the norm..."
"That's not me!"
"That's not him!"

Though *every* woman experiences it,
they still scream, "Not all men!".

It is your pastors,
kids' teachers;
it is husbands, fathers,
sons.

Your sisters are weeping
because we've all been there before.

It is the mailman
and the grocer,
the taxi driver,
and the CEO.

They exist in all places where women exist, where women go.

Women cannot walk alone
at night or in the day.
Women must protect their drinks, share their location, screen
their dates.

Even if it isn't *you*,
one man is too many;
and if you are not speaking up,
then you are still complacent.

Instead of calling us "man-haters"
because we speak our truth,
ask any woman that you know
how many times she has felt unsafe
whenever she encountered a man
who put himself in her space.

I'll wait…
.

.

.

So, fuck your silence,
it *is* all men
until it is no men at all.

Fuck your response of
"not all men", and
on those words,
I hope you
fucking choke.

Wicked Clouds

There is a storm brewing
far away in the distance,
but moving quickly, thundering,
and if you are quiet and listen,
you will hear the bats flying
to their caves for safety,
and the owls hooting
warning all the land of the hazy,
dark clouds moving with the wind,
the storm is growing closer now,
maybe I should go in...
though, Mother Nature calls to me,
I hope She is my friend,
and not an enemy
after Her revenge.
I take my chances, choosing
nature over shelter,
I want to see the beautiful sky
as Mother Nature passes by,
I just want to meet Her.
The clouds are getting darker now,
She is becoming quite wicked,
throwing Her lightning, spinning
Her funnels of wind,
spewing all of Her anger...
when will Her wrath end?
I connect with Her,
for She understands my rage,
just like I comfort in Hers.
The wicked Mother,
riding Her wicked clouds;
who will She take Her vengeance
out on first?

Tattered Hearts

My soul is spent,
withered, and bent.

Still, I get up, I go,
I try again.

How much more
can a depleted heart take?

How many times
can one heart break

before the glass is
completely shattered—

not just nicked, or worn,
or tattered?

May my absence
bring you peace;
may your actions
no longer drown me.

With these words,
I release you,
and reclaim a few of
my heart's pieces.

Amanda L. Ball

Sinister Merry-Go-Round

And we are all just hurting
each other
in this vicious game
we play;
a cycle that continues
when we don't get our way.

Jumping ropes
swung at our throats,
bouncing on the see-saw
of all of our emotions.
Feeding each other lies,
like there's not enough corrosion
in this world,
inside our homes,
on the news,
and in our phones.
We download the games that
we play with each other's minds,
with each other's kind...ness.
We take all the good ones
for granted.

It's an ongoing cycle
without an end,
this sinister merry-go-round
life that we live.

Yearning

We have been painted in this light for so long, they had no idea what we looked like in the dark.

They say we've all gone mad, like maybe witches really do exist, maybe they have given us a little too much freedom.

They didn't listen, not one time, while we screamed.

We were always asking for it; we just can't keep our legs together, maybe we should do better.

So, it's our fault when they rape, we had too much to drink...un-fucking-conscious;
dead.

They let their guard down and we got in their heads, and now we must pay, hung up on the stake.

Hearing their insults, feeling their stones...it stings... throwing in the gasoline...Karma, save me!

We were literally yearning for peace.

Theft of Universe

They say the full moon
drives women crazy,
turns us all into a witch—
at which time we hold hands,
sing—naked—and dance,
twirling around
when no men are found
to witness us all
entranced.

I would bathe nightly
under the moon
and dance with the
stars in the sky,
call out to Orion,
howl with the wolves,
and to the crows and ravens,
sing them lullabies goodnight.

But man is wicked;
stealing the universe
from women,
and until their evil is done,
we will be shunned
for trying to dance
in peace.

The Taking Tree

Once upon a time,
there was a tree,
and it took nourishment
from the earth.
It gathered the water
from rain,
and it flourished in the
sun's rays.

It grew and it grew,
and it wanted to
grow bigger,
so it took more earth,
more rain,
more sun;
its branches
sprouting freely,
its reign had just
begun.

It took the nearby
apple's seeds,
so it could have its own.
But the tree was never
satisfied.

It took some oranges,
peaches, and cherries,
then went to the
banana tree
and cut off all
its branches.

The orchards were
dying,
the people were
crying,
for no oak
can grow their
fruit.

But the tree
doesn't care,
even if it stays
bare,
it still owns
all the fruit
on the farm.

The famished people
are baffled,
they had worked so hard

to grow the trees,
to feed the needy,
to give everyone
fruit tarts.

Now the tree's greed
is blatant—
taking and taking—
until no other tree
is left.

As the people approach
with their saws
and their chains,
the tree knows
now it's too late
to give back what
it stole,
to save its own
soul,
as it hates and
it hates,
and it takes,
and it takes,
and it takes.

Haunted Carousel

Show your tickets,
step inside,
I know you are
dying to ride
the ponies,
and dragons,
the unicorns,
or stallions—
circling 'round
and 'round,
hiding their talons.
Yes, they do
appear sweet,
but what you
cannot see
is what is
waiting in the dark—
a nightmare of
which you'll be a part.
You must have missed it,
there on the ticket
in gold letters,
we did declare it.
You are now bound
to this jaunt,
an excursion that
will truly haunt
the paradise you
hoped you'd find
on this haunted
carousel ride.
Step right up,
the time is here;
there is no use
in fighting, I fear.

On the outside,
it looks like a dream,
but this haunted carousel
will make you scream.
No, you may not
exchange your ticket;
though, your other choices
are *not* as wicked.
Welcome to the
circus from hell,
it is time to ride
the haunted carousel!

The Storm is Coming

You say *feminist* like it's a bad thing,
like you don't know why I have
all this fucking rage,
like you haven't heard all of us scream.

You call me *woke*, like I'm supposed to be in the dark,
asleep,
like watching people suffer is your own, personal
movie.

You call me a *snowflake*, as if I melt as soon as I fall,
as if all of us together
don't form a fucking blizzard.

And the storm is coming...

The Webs We Weave

Like a spider,
taking my words
and stitching them together,
sewing a web of
wrath, of hunger...
a web of danger

The ravens and crows
circling overhead,
stalking and cawing...
unafraid of the web

As I weave my trap
to feed myself,
to fill the void
starvation left

I take my time
luring my prey
while the birds above
just want to take

And so, I keep watch
and sharpen my fangs,
for the daggers I bear
can cut off their wings.

Burning the Castle Gates

The Final Dinner

They eat their cakes,
and lobster,
and steaks,
drinking their whisky
and wine,
with no concern
for the rest of us
who are starving...
and dying while
they dine.

Ungrateful Bastards

Here we are, locked in our cages,
while they lie to us and steal our wages.
Self-made billionaire, they say,
though they obtained it from our pay.
Still they want more, it's never enough;
so they tax us again and threaten to take our stuff
if we do not bow, if we do not obey,
if they do not get their way.
And so we, the people, buy them cars,
fancy houses, jets, send them to the stars,
while we sit down here in the dirt
begging for a morsel of what we're worth.
They claim they will protect us
whether we like it or not,
misuse our bodies, claiming it's *their* choice.
They will not stop taking from us all,
expecting *us* to build the wall
that they will just hide behind,
feasting away while we die.
They claim to be helping—
it will all trickle down;
but we were lost to them long ago,
never to be found.
No help for the poor,
no help for the sick;
we're just ungrateful bastards
feeding the rich.

Behind the Shower Curtain

I just want to be free to be
who I have always been
behind the shower curtain...

where I can sing at the top of my lungs,
cleanse my body of the burdens of the world,
pretend for just a moment
that my mind is not filled with toil.

Scrub away all of the dirt,
forgetting about all of the hurt;
exfoliate all of the hate,
lather up and wash it away.

Behind the curtain, I can be
who I am truly meant to be,
when the outside world
cannot see me...so clearly.

I can be silly or I can be raw,
hair down the drain—goodbye, flaws;
cleanse my face of the worry,
taking my time, I'm in no hurry.

Behind the shower curtain,
I bask in the warmth
with no concern for
the outside world.

They will never see
all the secrets that I keep
when I am stripped bare,
while I'm washing my hair.

Maybe one day we will all be free
to be the person that we see
when we are our most true self,
before putting the towels back on the shelf.

The Girls Will Be Women

The boys are out playing,
the girls are inside,
watching from the kitchen
window

Boys throwing sticks
and fighting with fists,
and girls sipping on
tea

The boys wearing black, blue, and
maroon,
the girls in a pretty, pink
dress

The boys tell a joke
the girls don't know
as they call them
little women

The girls they grow
and they glow,
while the boys
grow quite slow

So, the boys are still boys
and the girls are their toys
even though they are underage
women

A Fool's Circus

Step right up and you will see
the greatest act in all the land—
flying monkeys, devious baboons,
lions and tigers leading prey to their den.

Do not be afraid to enter—
they are locked inside their cages;
this circus act is nothing new,
it's been around for ages.

You will witness—
on the flying trapeze—
men with huge egos,
throwing around women with ease.

Do not let it give you a fright;
this is the show you earn
when the fool's unite.

The clowns are suiting up now,
big red shoes, red hats, red noses;
this is what you all signed up for,
there will be no refunds for your purchase.

Watch closely now as the giant man
enters the arena with all your cash in hand.
This is no magic trick, he took it right from you
while you were distracted by the clown's shoes.

I know this isn't the spectacle
you had in mind
when you bought the tickets
and stood in line,

but we listed the acts
right there on the ads;
you must not have read it...
or must not have cared.

And so, the fools must also attend
this fool's circus until the very end.
Hold on tight, we're about to begin
the most foolish extravaganza
that has ever been.

Snakes in the Grass

They sneak around
as we pass by,
waiting for their time
to attack

While we listen to music,
look forward and behind,
hoping to not trip
on the cracks

They slither and hiss
with their tongues,
attempt to bewitch
us with their eyes

Walking through the garden gate,
we step in
and it's too late

We can't escape

They may not *all* be poisonous,
but they are still snakes.

Greed Goblins

Listen closely, children,
to what I have to say;
the gargoyles come out
at the end of the day.
They feed on the rats
and chase all the women,
they will steal children's youth
if we don't stop them.
They snatch up souls
and bathe in the holes
that were dug for our
coffins,
and we *still* haven't
stopped them.
We let them feast
while we waste away
on the cold, hard
ground.
Their hearts of stone
will break our bones
because that's what we
have allowed.
Hide in the sewers,
run into the trees,
save some rats as you flee.
They won't stop
until they own it all,
and we are almost
sold out.

Gaslighter

There you go again,
using my truth against me,
spreading your lies,
expecting me to believe them;
and when I don't,
you lose control—
the monster is coming out;
all you know how to do
is lie, and scream, and shout.
You call me the liar
though, you're the one on fire—
evidence of the fumes
ignited from you—the propellant—
just another gaslighter.

A Garden of Ash

Once a beautiful wonderland
of magical mushrooms
and fairies

filled with roses, and tulips,
and bushes growing
berries

The children frolicked
down the paths,
though that was long ago,

and since the fire spread,
the garden is no more

It was closed shut,
locked up tight,
peeping through
the keyhole
will give you a
fright

Spread around
all over the ground—
decay, and filth,
and rot

No one tends to the
garden,
no one seems to care,
all the passersby
forgot that it is there

Though rain comes and goes,
the garden doesn't grow,
for grass
doesn't sprout
through ash

If I could find the key
or scale the wall,
if someone would just
let me in

I could finally discover
the secrets of the garden
and stop living
in the
past

Beauty in the Beast

There is beauty in the beast
that those who fear
will never see.
They see sins and
wickedness;
they don't accept
those who are
different.
And they will
never understand
how the beast
came to be,
though, I will tell you
this story, so
listen carefully.

The beast was born
like you and I,
a tiny baby with
a mighty cry;
the beast was not
their name.
Though, as they grew
and learned to speak,
the people would never
let the beast be;
the beast was threatened,
convicted...
framed.

The beast had only
ever wanted love,
a happy fairytale ending;
but many stories of
happiness are just
people pretending.

The people hated *themselves*—
it was not truly the beast they
loathed;
they chose to turn their
hate on them, stripping
the beast bare—unclothed.

And as the beast was
standing there,
shivering from the cold,
the people saw
what they always missed—
the beast's beauty
now exposed.

Tucked within
the beast's dark skin,
the kindest, purest heart;
like the moon
at midnight, it lit up
the dark.

The people all mesmerized,
as they could not stop
from staring,
but the beast never before
allowed them to see,
knowing what they were
carrying.

The bright, beautiful heart
was not meant for this world,
and when human eyes
laid upon it,
they were placed into
a trance—a spell,
as the beast locked it
back up, forgotten.

Fortress

I seal myself off inside my
lair;
I prefer the dungeon—
underground,
buried.
No windows here, where I
can plot
and plan the next demise,
no one shall be
the wiser.
Inside their castle,
they would lock me in a
tower,
cutting off my long hair,
so I no longer have
power.
But here in my fortress,
I will decide...
who lives...and
who dies.
They are sure to attempt
to invite themselves
and break in,
though when they do,
I'll be prepared...
they may have their
fancy castles and steeds,
but it is them who should
be scared.
Here inside my fortress,
I will use my wicked heart
and all the blackest magic
to create my darkest art.

So, bring your soldiers
if you dare,
my canvas has been
wiped clean;
I need new bones
to construct more homes
for the witches out
on the street.

Demand, Defy, Defend

They call it violence
because they don't comprehend
oppression.
They call us angry
because *they* threatened our
safety.
They call us *woke*
because they don't have
empathy,
and they refused to take
accountability.
They call us victims,
though we are survivors,
and they failed to see
that we are so fucking tired
of being held back,
being left to starve
while they fly their jets
and golf in their backyards.
Though, we were refused access,
we have tried to be patient,
begging for the most basic
of human kindness.
The oppressed can only
take so much
before we defy
unjust rulers.
And so we shall defend
the spaces we belong in,
and will demand
a seat at the table;
and if we are denied...
just remember,
we tried.

Your Worst Nightmare

You thought it was funny—
those jokes about our bodies.
You thought we owed you—
an unspoken contract.
And then you spew threats
anytime you don't get
exactly what you wanted.

You've heard of Freddy
wreaking havoc on Elm Street,
but your nightmares are
where we will soon meet.

I will slide into the shadows
of your haunted dreams,
waiting for the perfect
moment to make you scream.

I will be waiting
around every corner
ensuring each night
your mind will be tortured.

I will transform myself into your
every wish, a beauty—magnificent,
then feed you toxic apples
just like Maleficent.

If you believe that women
who identify as feminists
are a threat, just wait
till we become misandrists.

It may be too late
for you to change
your toxic mind
and toxic ways...

Go right ahead,
keep on berating,
for I will be
right here waiting.

I will write the story
about your ongoing horror
until your soul breaks and bleeds,
then, I will call the coroner.

The Sound of Violence

Shut off the noise,
turn down the spite,
lower the anger, and
release the hate

the savagery is deafening,
the abhorrence is loud

the malice is frightening,
increasing the sound

cut off the resentment,
chop down the bitterness,
swallow the vitriol, and
spit out the venom

lay down your swords,
the brutality is shattering
and your ruthlessness knows
no kind of boundaries

tune it all out,
it's all too loud;
give me the silence
over the sound
of violence.

Inside the Mind of the Storm

There are storms
inside my head
brewing
and swirling,
endless dread.

Sometimes they transform
into beautiful words
so carefully placed,
so wonderfully churned.

Sometimes they are spewed
with rage-filled anger,
desperate to be heard,
grasping for just one ounce
of calmer water.

Other times they are gentler,
a soft breeze from my lips,
comforting, warming, though
it's not long before I slip

back into the angst,
into the fire—
fueling the flames.

I can't keep them inside
or I would eventually
combust,
and so I let them out
before I am crushed

with all of the heaviness
my chest can manage;
I have to try
not to panic.

And so, I pour them
into my words,
into my ink,
a beautiful verse.

I tucked them away
for so very long,
allowing no one
to hear my song.

But storms can be beautiful,
Mother Nature angers, too;
and the Universe always gifts
us
sleep with the Moon.

Street Party

He thought I was weak
when he passed me on the street...
because I was all alone.
I was walking hastily,
late for my party,
and he chose to walk
right in front of me.
As he smirked at me
and called me *baby*,
I refused to move out of his way,
for he knew he walked into *my* path...
with all of his audacity,
as I bumped into him and
he stumbled back.
I took my opportunity
as he fumbled around
to retrieve my blade
and leave him bleeding
on the ground.
They think we are weak
because we are women,
they think we won't fight back.
But we've witnessed this toxicity
since we were little...
and now we're ready
to attack.

Church Fire

I asked for forgiveness,
I asked to be set free
from all of the burdens
and angst
laced inside of me.

They called me a sinner,
they called me a whore;
they don't understand
what forgiveness is for.

I begged for mercy,
I pleaded for peace,
please take these demons
entrapping me.

I got on my knees,
I prayed to their lord;
they told me it wasn't
enough.

They ripped me up,
peeled me from the floor
and evicted me from their
church.

I clawed at the doors
outside—
scratches, long and deep,
I screamed bloody murder;
someone, please save me!

The ghosts are haunting,
the demons stirring,
they've awakened from their
nest.

I won't have any control
once they take over
my soul,
and they
will never
rest.

I drank the blood
and I ate your offerings;
I sang all the right songs,
I read the words
that said my soul was worth
fighting for.

But you've closed me out,
you've shut me down,
and the devil offered me
a cure.

She'll take this heavy, aching
soul,
she'll strip it from my body
if I just do this one, small
task,
it's really a small favor to
ask...

She barters with me
while I scream
and try to break down your
door,

but you only listen
to the other Christians
who don't know what
I'm good for.

You call *me* a sinner,
you call *me* a liar...

locked up in your steeple
with all the lost people...

as the devil conspires
with all of the fire
I keep trapped inside...

and as I lust
for someone to trust,
I finally combust...

church fire!!

Bone Garden

We built our houses
and made them homes,
planted the herbs,
the roses...the thorns.
We watered them daily
and enjoyed our harvest.
We shared with our
neighbors,
we loved one another;
we worked hard to live in
peace.

The trolls came knocking,
demanding favors,
demanding a portion
of what we had grown.
We—politely—told them *no*.

They wouldn't listen
and brought in assistance
to terrorize our world.
Our beautiful homes and
gardens
torn to shreds,
for no one denies a troll's
tolls.

We owed them nothing,
and still they expected
for us all to do as we're told.

And so we promised them
payment
so we could live
safely...alone...

So, under that notion,
we mixed our potions,
and invited them back into
our homes...

We only wanted to plant our
garden...

and now it will be full of
their bones.

Medusa

The king and all his soldiers
had locked the women out,
barricaded the doors from
within,
and chained up all of the
gates.

The women were begging—
the gardens are all inside;
what are we to do
if we cannot find any food?

And so, they searched
far and wide, until
they came across a cave...

A woman lived
deep inside,
who gave them quite
a fright.

Her lair was full of snakes—
on the ground and on her
head—
they turned back quickly,
but stopped once she said

she had been in their
shoes before,
exiled, left to die

and she may be able
to assist...she was willing
to fight.

And so, the women
marched right back
to storm the castle
gates.

And when the men eyed
Medusa, they were turned
to stone by her snakes.

Now it was time to break
down
the walls, to reclaim what
was
theirs.

With Medusa on their side,
the men never stood
a chance.

Gas Masks

They're killing us
with their greed,
with their
bribery

They're killing us
with their toxic fumes
of rage and power
and control

We are outside
rattling the gates,
storming them,
climbing them

We could really get in.
Together.
Hold my hand!

Come on, stand!

We charge.

Together.

They're killing us
while they're in there
feasting
on steak, and ham,
and wine

throwing us the bones
outside

They want a barbecue?
We can give them one.

Smoke them out,
then...
have our fun.

They Were Asking for It

They cheated
and stole;
they bribed
and they lied.
They hoarded it all,
the jewels...
and the food.
They locked it all up
inside their castles,
set their dragons
upon us
to turn us
to ashes.
They swam in the
money they gained
from our labor
and told us all
it was self-made.
But all of their crimes
are written in their eyes
and it's too late for them
now.

Grab your pitchforks,
bring your neighbors,
light your torches.
Tonight, we will take it back
or set fire to it all
and scorch it.

Burning the Castle Gates

They locked us out long enough,
thinking if they starve us, it won't be tough
to beat us, overpower us,
defeat us...

Though, we came together today,
combined our resources,
made extra plates...
no longer famished

Now hydrated—and angry—
we grab our torches,
ready to scorch it,
no time to waste

Gather matches and gasoline,
lanterns, and lighters,
set fire
to the castle gates!

Wicked Dreams Goodnight

Feasting on the Bones

The Bones of My Youth

Oh, to be young again,
splashing through puddles,
and sprinklers, and rain
with a smile on my face.

Now, the clouds come out
and I nearly drown,
holding on and
pulling myself from the brink
of death.

It's just rest

that I need,

a bit more sleep,

my bones are weak.

Climbing the jungle gym
and doing cartwheels
in the grass
on a hot summer day
making lemonade,
riding my bike
no hands
don't stop.

My bones were strong
once before.

My mind grows
while my bones wither,
and the soul knows
all the cracks
I've left hidden,
covering them up,
concealing them,
buried deep.

My bones feel it all,
carrying the weight
of a soul that forgot

what it means
to be seen,
to dream.

Instead, the bones break.

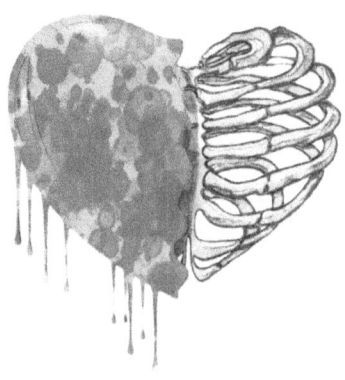

What Do I Owe Her?

There must be a price, an amount,
we can agree on.
I poured my soul out to her,
every ounce, empty now;
still, it's not enough.

I drank from her cup,
accepted her love,
offered mine...
"In due time..."
though never, ever enough.

Anxiously waiting to discover
what she wants from me
in return for my
earthly bones.
I loved her!

Still, she pushes me around,
twisting my words,
juggling my hurt...
oh, please, Universe!

What more do I owe you?!

A Vampire's Heart

My makers didn't seem to
care
when I was turned vampire,
that I loathe the taste of
blood,
and so, the ritual transpired.

And here I am, waking
from a long slumber,
rising from my casket
with an awful hunger.

The dirt and filth
beneath my nails
reminds me that
I fought like hell

to keep from turning
into what they made me,
so, it's their fault
that I've gone crazy.

Under the moon,
I howl and scream,
as they point, and
judge, and demean—

a useless vampire who
rejects immortality,
an outcast monster
who loathes brutality.

Though, this is who
I have become,
no longer allowed
to walk in the sun.

Forced to live with
a soul turned dark,
now that I have
a vampire's heart.

Skeletal Sadness

The busy-ness of the day
has settled, like dew on grass,
and night is now creeping in,
extending its long fingers out
toward me, as my mind
finally has time
to wander.

I am all shut in, swaddling myself
in thoughts of...everything.
What was...what is...
what could be...
covered in ideas,
in a comfort

of sadness and awe and woe;
my weary body and adventurous
mind, dancing in an epic battle
where the only loser
is my soul—
consumed, overwhelmed,
inspired, tired.

My body craves rest...a peaceful,
dreamless sleep, where my mind
won't keep it tossing and turning
and yearning.

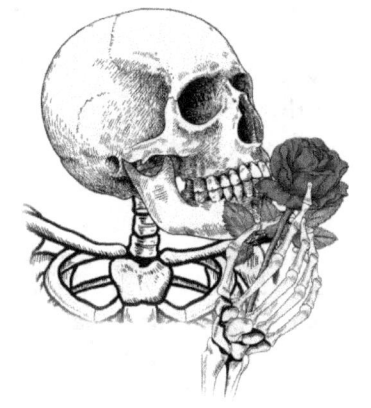

My soul the essence, my heart
the angel, my mind the devil
struggling, pulling,
taking control

as I sift through all this madness
buried in this
skeletal sadness.

Hopeless Dreams

We are all down here starving,
trying to bribe and to bargain
for an easier existence
while the greedy are being persistent.

They keep taking and asking for more,
while they get richer and we get poor;
our very souls are at war—
with good and evil—which we can't afford.

I'm not sure how much more resilience
I can muster for this resistance,
feeling locked inside a prison,
we are all just begging for assistance.

Robin Hood was the true vigilante,
though, his methods were uncanny,
he did his part to keep the poor steady
on this rollercoaster life, sometimes heavy.

It is far past time for greed
to become non-existent, so we may be freed
from the chains that we never agreed
to be bound to—a hopeless dream?

Will we ever get a say
in this game that they play;
will we ever find a way
to no longer be afraid

of the rules we never wrote,
forced to live with and to hope
that all of us can cope
with this noose wrapped around our throats?

An endless cycle of fear and dread,
every day when we get out of bed,
hoping that one day we will shed
all of the burdens floating in our heads.

Stained Wishing Well

The Wishing Well was swirling
black
sending all the tossed coins
back;
a penny landed in my
eye
and I got thrown into a
fight.
No matter that you're
innocent,
this Wishing Well is not
elegant.
It's swirling black with
lust, with hate
for all the souls lost
along the way.
The wishes of bribery,
lies, and cheats
were more than the Wishing Well
could take.
And so, we are being refunded all
of our coins
and showered with all of the angst
and the toil.
We shall carry it with us
wherever we go
if the wishes aren't for the
starving people
below.

Burnt Crust

It's been overcooked, yet again,
covered in an encrustation.
Like a scab stuck on the skin,
we left it ablaze for too long.

Released from the fire,
waiting to cool,
a hardened crust
surrounds torched food.

It's hard to be picky
when your stomach is empty;
it's hard to take pity
when we've all been forgotten.

They walk around denying
this incinerated furnace
we are all living in
here on earth's surface.

They claim the cold weather
proves them right,
even as wildfires spread
and innocent life dies.

But don't you worry, they can afford
to move to a new planet—the moon or mars,
while the rest of us spin on this
burnt crust and get charred.

We are all dying in this fire,
we will all be scorched;
as we throb and ache in pain,
and they throw us another torch.

The Clowns are Coming!

They're coming in numbers,
piling up in their cars,
stuffed in with each other
while the world falls apart.

They're joking and clowning,
one great, big act,
then they look disappointed
when we don't laugh.

And so, they turn angry—
clowns with damaged egos,
they strip us of happiness
and we have no vetoes.

Then they dance a little
more,
expecting us to praise them;
though, it is impossible to
smile
when we are being
condemned

to a life we didn't sign up
for—
a circus act for the ages.
If only this was just a story
written within a book's
pages.

But, alas, this is the act
we are all stuck watching
together,
looking around at all the
clowns
dragging us through this
endeavor.

Maybe it is finally time
to free the animals from their
cages,
release the giant elephants,
as the tigers start raging.

Set flames to the tents
they've got us trapped in,
burn it all down, this
unhinged carnival they're
exacting.

The clowns are coming!
We're running out of time.
Now we must all witness
their heinous crimes.

Try to save the children
as you flee,
though, I think I'll stay and
watch
them trip over their own
clown feet.

Amanda L. Ball

The Skulls of My Enemies

I wake from a days' long slumber,
mouth parched, my stomach angry
with hunger.

My body must have been exhausted
after fighting through all the torment;
my soul also spent.

I was meant for compassion and softness,
not whatever *this* life is—this planet
not suited for my tenderness.

And so, I had to hide away my benevolence;
though, in the dark I hold on to kindness.
After too much destruction, I lost my tolerance.

It was time to pull out my vengeance;
no more reprieve for the
immoral inequalities.

A new day is here, and it's time
to drink my tea
from the skulls of all
my enemies.

I Deserve a Little Treat

I've worked so hard—
took all the right paths
to leave my anger
in the past.

I moved on,
I let it go—
all the damage done
to my impaired soul.

I've patched it up,
restored the light,
and now it glistens
in the night.

It wasn't easy—
healing never is—
my perseverance,
my lifelong gift.

They keep trying
to tear me down,
though I keep floating—
I can't be drowned.

Each time I show
a piece of my soul,
they swoop in to vandalize
my home.

They refuse to leave
me in peace,
and so I deserve
a little treat.

They may view
my soul as black,
but it is their hearts
that are my favorite snack.

The Mad Chatter

It's time for tea again,
the same old shit,
another day.

Wake up,
coffee,
clock in...

I'd rather climb
back in
to my
coffin.

But the palace wants
its taxes
and I'm late again.

One shouldn't haste
or delay
when the Queen
wants heads on a
plate.

There's no time to
chase rabbits
or chat
with cats
speaking to you
from a tree.

No matter
that you've gone
mad,
more chatter
inside your head.

One lump or two?
No, that won't do...

There is no time for tea.

Warning Alert

They walk around the streets
of the city,
greed in their pockets,
seeping through
into their skin.

They shake hands with
each other,
spreading their disease
while the rest of us
scream.

We are dying—
our children at school
and by police—
no one to trust.

So we scream.

More taken away,
left to bleed
because my body is not worth
any more than a fetus...
or...
the dirt.

And so, we scream.

They get home and take off
their greed clothes
and they replace them
with their rape robes.

And they turn on their TVs,
drinking their fancy scotch,
kick off their shoes,
turn on the news

and don't understand what
they did
to deserve this—
being gunned down
just walking down
the street

like they haven't heard us

fucking scream.

Amanda L. Ball

The Witches' Revenge

They threw their stones
and yelled vile things,
as they tied her up
and set her to flames.

They watched her burn
as she screamed,
then walked away and
wiped their hands clean.

Though, you cannot destroy
a witch's soul,
and all that evil of man
soon takes a toll.

The witches who were scorched,
tortured, and drowned
are returning again
to that demented town...

They're marching in numbers—
cauldrons in tow—
chanting their curses,
making it known

that when you play with fire,
you, too, will get burned.
What you do to others
will one day be returned.

As they storm the evil town,
and gently place their cauldrons down,
incanting their hexes without a sound;
with their spells, the wickedness shall drown.

As the monstrous people beg for mercy,
the witches cackle diabolically,
stirring and brewing,
their potions stewing...

with their sorcery of charms,
the witches exact their revenge;
and now they're flying out on their brooms
whittled from the bones of men.

Ashtray

It's time to smoke them out;
we've waited long enough,
sitting here in fear,
their time has finally come.

We asked for peace,
though they didn't agree,
and so now we...
shall invade *their* territory,
as they have always
invaded ours.

I do not condone violence,
but I cannot stand the silence,
and so fight with us
or behind us,
but we will march on.

And when we are done,
we can celebrate
smoldering all of their hate,
light our matches
to burn our cigarettes
filled with their ashes.

Long, slow drag...
it tastes evil in here;
let's put it out.

Black Cats Attack

The witch's best friend
is the agile black cat,
scaling walls
ten feet tall
sneaking in for the
attack.

The witches wait patiently
outside with their brooms
while their black cats
hunt inside the rooms—
gathering mice and rats,
building an army of bats.

They can infiltrate the castle quietly,
but even if they are caught,
they may be mistaken for a stray,
shooed away, or even
offered a home.

You see, witches don't need
a Trojan horse to slip into the
castle walls;
black cats will do their bidding,
and then gnaw on all of
the bones.

A Murder of Crows

A crow is a familiar
to the young witch
learning spells,
brewing potions,
deadly notions,
the chants she knows
so well.

She searches for her coven,
the crow guiding her from high,
as the other witches
find her in the night.

And as the familiar crows
gather on branches overhead,
they learn from the witches,
and form their own plans.

The witches chant for hope—
they chant for peace,
though, the crows have witnessed
all the wickedness
of the world outside
these trees.

Once the witches have gone home,
tucked inside their cottages, and
covered up their bones,

the crows return into the night,
causing quite a shudder,
eviscerating all the depravity;
after all, they were named a *murder*.

Basking in the Blood

I tried to be nice,
to put on a smile,
to say all the right words.
I used *please* and *thank you*,
and *yes ma'am* and *sir*,
though what I did
was never enough.
And since I stopped trying,
they started crying,
calling me all the names
in the book.
I let it all fuel me,
like sunlight on a fire—
ready to burst.
Now, I have a campfire
to cook up my dinner
and bask in the blood
seeping into the earth.

Man Eater, Man Hater

She's been called a *man-hater*
since she stood up for herself;

they didn't know
that when she goes home,
she feeds on the blood
from their souls.

Though, when men are vicious
they become quite delicious,
filled with anger-pumped hearts,
sweet and tasty like tarts
and she
swallows them
whole.

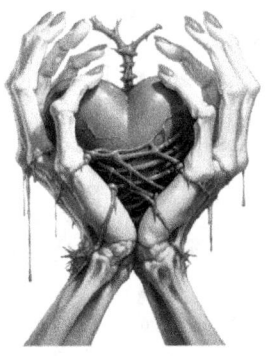

Tell her to smile at you
and she will attack you
and turn you into
a stew.

So, call her a bitch,
but she's actually that witch
you kept turning her
into.

Cookbook

I write in the night—
my mind blocked in the light
of the day, the sun
beaming bright.

If it's not dark or cloudy,
my thoughts not heavy,
my pen gets stuck,
my ideas unsteady.

Within the day
I could write about gentler things,
though it's the grave
words that soothe my soul.

If I begin
to go easy on evil men
and no longer write about
their endeavors,
then they would win—
women not heard—
and we would all be tethered

to their darkness—their depravity—
chained under their control
for a few more centuries;

and that simply will not do...

And so, I choose my weapon—
the pen, allow my anger to brew,
wait for the night,
hide out of sight,
and write a cookbook
for my favorite men stews.

Dinnertime!

You judge our bodies—
too fat, too thin,
too straight, too curvy,
too fake, too real.

You underestimate our
intelligence—
too weak, you think,
assuming we won't
take our place

where we belong in society;
you believe we are not
strong enough to hold
power or authority.

Men have forgotten
that women are more cunning,
more witty, more witchy,
and always becoming

stronger and wiser,
uplifting each other,
fueling the fire

where we can sit around together
turning into witchy sinners...
no, I may never be thinner
because I eat men like you for dinner.

Toothpicks

They feast their eyes
upon us—salivating—
as we shiver;
dirty eyes and hands
roaming
where we never asked
them to go.
They're after our bodies,
trying to damage our souls.
They thought they could
break us,
leave us meeker
and weaker.
They just didn't know
we eat men like them
for dinner.

Join me, ladies,
gather round,
the table is set for us all.
My heart is parched,
my mouth is drooling
for a bite.
Who needs utensils,
we'll use our hands,
pass around the meat.
Sip their blood
from our cups,
and use their bones
to pick our teeth.

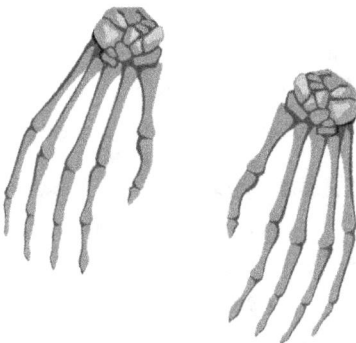

Feasting on the Bones

We burned their castle to the ground,
set fire to their homes and towns,
we rallied, fought, stumbled,
and bled, and we shall now
be fed.

We will build our table a little bigger,
make space for all the hungry
children, and dine with fancy
teas and cakes, eat until our
stomachs ache.

I haven't felt satisfied
like this in quite a while,
what was that delicacy,
what's in that dish;
have the rich always tasted
as good as this,
or is that my long term hunger
causing me such a blunder?

I think I need to lie down
at home
after feasting on
all of their bones.

Wicked Dreams Goodnight

Dancing on the Graves

Bury the Coffin

Digging through dirt
underneath gravel,
my hands callused
and torn.

Here I go,
this again,
my morbid
ever after.

Midnight strikes,
running out of time,
the full moon has risen.

Haunted by
the ghosts outside,
not the ones
within

the cemetery

I'm digging in.

Hitting rocks,
wearing down
the skin
I must shed,

so I can escape
what's outside the gates
and stay in the shadows,
hidden.

Digging my home
to bury my bones
I no longer have
any use for.

Extract my soul,
take it whole,
so the casket
I will fit in.

Watch Your Back

I am the witch and the angel;
I tell you what to do.
Sometimes it's sweet, uplifting,
but, alas, I switch, and then
it's wicked.
Blood boiled over,
temperature rising;
can't put out this fire
inside me.
Chant my hexes,
sing my spells,
calm my soul,
so the wings can
swell.
Take a curtsy,
twirl my dress,
remind you that
you need to rest.
Though the sweet
cannot last
when the witch is
always
on your
back.

The Goddess, Karma

Strip me
Beat me
Shame me
Frame me
Use me
Abuse me
What good am I for?

You want me to bare my soul,
to pour all of me onto the floor,
so you can trample upon my temple,
my body no longer
whole.

You use my body—
it's only a tool—
and you pray to the god
who gave me to you.

But your god is wicked,
you've been led astray.
And my goddess is angry
when my freedom's at stake.

Demeaning
Belittling
your treacherous words
only add fuel
to the fight,
to our cause.

Women are used to being torn down,
to being stripped bare,
thrown to the ground.

Women are also used to taking our time,
plotting and scheming,
planning our crimes.

While men are breathing,
women are prey.
While women give breath,
we can take it away.

Karma's a sister.
Karma's a friend.
Karma won't stop
until we're all safe
from men.

Reveling for Peace

We do not celebrate the end of a life.
We are not jumping for joy over
someone's demise,
though, some comfort is implied...

innocent people have been dying
and they want us crying
over leaders who have been denying
medicine for the sick...the ailing.

Elderly withering away in the cold,
children and women being sold
to the highest bidder paying the toll,
and we are still being told

that billionaires do not pay their share,
and Goddess forbid that we dare
to ask them for a morsel more
to feed ourselves...and the poor...

...such venomous greed,
and yet we are called terrorists when we scream.
I do not see the need
to ever, ever retreat

until we can fully defeat
all of the liars and the cheats
who cannot even see,
or maybe do not believe,

in their own ability
to decrease
the problems of the world
with ease.

Tell me, please...

what is so wrong about dreaming
for peace?

And so, if I need,
I will continue to scream,
thanking the Goddess for relief
as the money hoarders—
the souls of thieves—
of this world are finally
released.

Grave Digging

One for me,
two for him;
one for women,
two for men.

Grave digging holes
for all of the coffins,
for all of the bodies,
for all of the dead men.

One each for the women
that they killed;
two for each man whose
fate is now revealed.

Vigilante Annie
digging graves,
the hearts of men
is all she craves.

When they're dead,
they can't rape.

Vigilante Annie digging
two holes
for all the toxicity
from their souls.

Grave digging for bodies,
grave digging for souls;
we don't recycle trash
around these parts.

Amanda L. Ball

The Madness We Keep

We tuck it away,
slide it into our pockets,
out of sight,
out of reach—
all but forgotten.

Though, we feel it there,
rubbing against our skin
with every step we take,
still trying to keep it tucked away.

Nearing the edge of a ledge
we thought we walked away from—
turned around, misguided,
a simple mistake...

and our souls, they ache.

So, we peer over—just a glimpse
is all we need...
what could be there
waiting for me?

My soul holding up my bones,
tired, weak...
and still it holds...on
a little longer.

There are black cats to pet
and poetry to write
and a moon to bask under

and still we wonder

why we are all going mad here...

He Had It Coming

Oh, the rich man was killed,
gunned down in the streets,
just walking along
minding his business...
what was he wearing?

Oh, the man was attacked,
car set ablaze
by a traitor...
how much did he have to drink?

Oh, the man who never
took *no* for an answer
had his prized jewels
snipped—taken...
why didn't he keep his legs closed?

Oh, the man was cut open
left to bleed
on the streets...
what did he do to deserve it?

The Witching Hour

The whispers in the wind
are the witch's friend,
guiding her through
the trees,
towards the full moon
where her friends dance
around in a
joyous mood.
She'll take their hands
and join in,
laughing, chanting,
and hexing...
until gone are all
the men.

Macabre Midnight

The dance of death was soon to begin,
grisly disturbances
filling the silence.

In the graveyard, we shall tread,
aiming to wake the dead,
as the skeleton guides us.

Keeping up with its every stride,
we romp and stomp as we follow behind—
a morbid picture to fill your mind.

Though, what they did was vile and loathsome;
so, now we shall make a toast by their tombstones.
I know it sounds extra gruesome;
don't be repulsed, they did deserve it.

This morbid party may sound repugnant—
their wasted lives such a misfortune.

We celebrate in grotesque ways
because our Goddess loves it...
and maybe so do we.

Grave dancing may be a dreadful sight;
though, we do not mean to give you a fright.
We commemorate burying the bones
of so many heinous souls—
our own macabre midnight.

The Villain's Story

The witches—the villains—
that we all know
are said to have
the darkest souls.

Misleading the people,
wreaking havoc on their path,
chanting their curses,
spreading their wrath.

Though, the story that you
often do not hear
is that the villains
have had plenty to fear.

The people have threatened
and labeled them dangerous
so many times,
their hearts now spent.

The villains were not
born this way;
they were forced
to claim their space

after they were exiled,
shut out, left to die;
the villains never
knowing why.

The exiled villains
had no choice
but to live or die,
and so, they were forced

to turn their souls
to the dark...
others never seeing all of the
beauty in their darkest parts.

An Abomination

Wearing her red dress,
slit thigh-high,
black, leopard heels,
smoky eyes,
turning the heads
of every guy
when she walks
into a room,
sparkling, dazzling,
va-va-voom!
Strutting on by,
looking for her table,
waiter!
yes, this way, miss...
her lady waiting,
sitting there,
in a black, lace dress;
time stands still...
men, they wilt
and cry,
oh, why
did we not get
an invitation,
can we sit?
Oh no, not here,
we're together...
and after some
hesitation...
they claim the beauties
an abomination

simply because
who they love
is sexier, softer,
gentler,
kinder,
stronger,
wiser,
women are fire!

Dancing with the Devil

The Devil says take him
home tonight.
The Angel says you're not
ready yet.

The Devil, she flirts and bats
her eyes.
The Angel says
"Not tonight".

The Devil wears heels and
that
little black dress,
while the Angel stays covered
up tight.

The Devil starts dancing,
drinking,
and romancing,
and the Angel tries to put up
a fight.

The Devil, she's angry—
a woman scorned.
The Angel still wants to cry.

The Devil straightens the
Angel's crown
and pulls her into
the night.

The Devil, she's done;
she's seen enough.
The Angel won't let
her be.

So she takes out
the lighter,
sets flames to
his tires
and winks as she
walks away.

The Devil is mad.
The Angel is sad,
and she's just lost
as can be.

But fuck those
tearful nights,
those lonely
cries;
fuck the way
he made
her feel.

He wounded the Angel
and woke up the Devil,
so she's ready to make
a deal.

The Devil sets out
to take him down
while the Angel cries
for peace.

Autumn Rising

The cool, crisp air riding
in the breeze,
pushing that last bit of summer
straight to its knees

the spirits and ghouls are rising
from their long slumber—
from inside their graves;
they're coming in numbers

the spookiest time for souls
to reunite as wistful ghosts
and all the saddest people
can feel a bit more at home

when pumpkins and apple cider
warm our cold, dark souls,
and graveyard parties pull us in
to dance with all the bones

when the leaves are changing
and the bats fly through the night...
my haunted soul is aching
for autumn to rise.

Black Magic

When you throw magic spells
into the wishing wells,
the dark will soon
take over.

Black as night,
the dreams inside
will be getting their
own makeover.

And now, little dolls
have transformed
into skulls,
and action figures
start to attack.

Girls and boys
running from their
toys,
and the witches,
they all
laugh.

Toss in a penny,
make your wish,
you can't take it
back;
the deed is done,
and now the fun
begins when the
magic is black.

Darkest Child

She always knew it was there
tucked inside, from another place;
she felt it; she fought it—
smile pretty, now

It would come out when
anger called, a simple chat
with a friend, a long lost muse

She felt it like fire, embers sparking
inside of her, smelling the fumes,
like her own custom perfume

She wore it, concealed under the fancy,
expensive fragrance, hiding it, a cloak;
she often hid it so well

But as the story goes, the battle
waged on, and there was no way to know
how this ending would go

And the war raged—the cannonballs
inside her, booming, crashing,
burning, dying

She picked herself up off the battlefield,
the shell of her lying there,
scattered into a thousand pieces

She's put bigger puzzles together before,
she is sure, she can solve this riddle,
she can mend her...self

Placed on a shelf too long, porcelain
is not a toy, and so she kept it there,
too afraid to touch

So, she viewed it from afar, wandering
into stories she could tell, if she could just
look inside

A peek...

an impulsive decision.

It was too late now.

Black Roses

Tucked away,
in the secret garden,
a tiny plant in soil
hidden behind a bush.
It looked as if it had died
a long, long time ago,
but I still wanted to
have a look.
As I got nearer,
thorns appeared
to grow bigger
and sharper,
covered in blood.
Oh, who would have
attacked
such a helpless creature,
an innocent plant forced
to defend its secrets?
And so, I nursed it
back to health,
watered it, saved it
from all it had been dealt.
I visited her every day,
hoping desperately
she would be okay.
I brought her gifts
and sang her songs;
for *all* life deserves
love, after all.
Finally, one day
in spring,
I showed up
to bring her
a drink...

I gasped loudly;
to my surprise,
she emerged from her cocoon
like a butterfly—
sprouting and flowering,
grown and towering
over the entire garden.
How did a tiny,
damaged plant
become a giant bush
of black roses?
As she smiled,
she waved to the ground...
her enemies' bodies
were finally decomposing.

Cemetery Play Date

Inside the cemetery where
I feel the most alive,
walking amongst the dead,
getting tucked in
to my dark, earthy bed;
singing lullabies, to the
corpses, goodnight,
wicked dreams,
let the vampires bite;
don't forget to brush
your fangs, and get
tucked in to your bat cave;
if you shall die before the day
I'll meet you in the cemetery to play.

Goodnight, Demons

I made love to the devil
as I bathed in my sin,
powdered my nose
with all the lost souls
and water-turned-wine
staining my lips

I thirst on the energy
I extract from the
killings;
I soak up the blood—
like a sponge—
of my enemies,

and pick my teeth...
with the bones
of the men
. . .
They threw me down here
and now cower knowing that I'm
home sweet home here;
I *can* make a dungeon
a home
. . .
I put out the fire,
doused with blood dripped
from my anger;
I take off for bed,
pull my soul-stitched robe
over my head,
kiss my demons
sweetly
goodnight

Bewitching

You pull me in to the song,
dancing as we sing along.
Smiling and laughing, twirling around,
you could bewitch me without a sound.

In your eyes I appear to be
mesmerizing, magical, captivating.
And in mine, I see you—
a comforting space where love is true.

May we always build blanket forts
and never stop stealing each other's hearts;
may we always dance at night
and bathe in each other under moonlight.

May your magic always uplift me
and keep me centered and living freely;
and may my own enchantments
forever leave you utterly breathless.

And if I shall die before you do,
I just might put a spell on you,
so that you may continue to enjoy your stay
until we meet again in our graves.

Divination

As we gather here tonight
under the moon's vibration,
our auras align
as we seek divination.

We light up our sage
to snuff out our rage,
exhausted from combat
against all of the autocrats.

We seek purer vibes,
a calming ambience,
as we reach into the sky
knowing we are more sapient

than the traitors
and dictators
that led us into the dark.

May our tranquil
elements combine
in a pattern of harmony
and fill up the night.

May our tarot show us
something more divine—
a sacred future
we enchant to find.

Oh, Mother Goddess,
will you dare to foretell—
is our fortune heavenly,
or is it pure hell?

We seek out your
foreboding,
and we feel your hesitation;
please guide us on the path
to a peaceful divination.

Graveyard Party

You are cordially invited
to an informal gathering
to celebrate the old and the new,
where you can leave behind
your unbearable disguise,
and come as you are
to dance under the moon.

On this night, we shall
bury the bones
of all of the men who
have wronged us.

Please confirm, don't hesitate,
invite your friends,
and don't be late;
the coven waits for no one.

We shall dine,
and we shall dance,
drinking wine, and
holding hands,
the stars and moon
our witness.

Don't forget to RSVP
to our annual midnight
graveyard party.

Dancing on the Graves

And so, we danced, and sang,
and praised
each other through the
darkest days;
we made it here, we're alive,
and we shall celebrate tonight.

The moon is high, the stars,
they glisten;
if you speak softly, and then
listen,
you will hear the coyotes howl,
the ravens caw,
the crows claw...
at the trees, at the ground,
dancing with us in perfect union,
I never want this night to end.
Sip our potions from the cauldron,
commemorate this night,
this day...
we shall now forever reign
supreme—the matriarchy—
dancing on their graves.

Howling at the Moon

Reclaiming Our Universe

They call us wicked,
though they are the thieves—
the filthy, depraved,
their souls made of teeth...
eating our bones,
torturing our souls,
while we gasp and beg
for peace.

They pilfered our stars
straight from the sky,
they lassoed, and roped up
our moon.
They poached the very earth
from beneath our feet
and chopped down
all of our trees.

They call us wicked,
so that's what we shall be.
If we want peace, we must claim it,
declare our victory...
taking back what is rightfully ours
so we may live harmoniously.

The universe was made for femininity,
and they refuse to let us be the
women—the essence—
we were always meant to be.

And so, it is past time
to take it all back,
have them groveling
on their knees.

They've had their fun
for generations...

we'll send them back
to where they belong
buried deep in the earth
under our feet.

Feast on their flesh,
drink of their blood,
dine until we are stuffed...

and leave the other pieces to
recycle...regrow...rebirth.

An Ode to Your God

He who is worthy,
get on your knees,
bow your head,
for I wear the crown.
And you must
please
me,
for I am king...

.

He tells his people
that it's all love,
then they show up
with their judgements
and shove
their anger and hate
right in our face.
They say
their book
conveys
that it's not okay
to love who we love.

.

To help the poor,
the needy and broken,
that is what He has spoken...

.

They say
their book
is truth,
but what they
preach
they don't do,
and then they
question
why we hate
religion,

why we don't trust
their preachers
or church.

.

And so we pave
a different
way
with acceptance
and kindness,
helping our sisters...

building our tables
to feed more people
and wondering if their God
is here where we are,
or if He's disgusted
with all of their judgements.

.

And so, I pray
for each
God's sake,
that you steer your people
back to your steeple...

because they got lost,
forgot who you were

if you ever
were there

at all.

Words Are My Therapy

Bathe me in them,
douse me—covered—
buried

Read them to me...softly,
warmly...sweetly

Comfort me in them,
as they roll off your tongue
onto my soul

Gift them to me, over and
over again
let me in
to read them all
from your skin

Let me taste them,
nourish my body,
fill me up again—
less depleted...
no longer starving

Satisfied.
My Zen.

And let them carry me through
again
again
again.

Hardcore Glitter

It is hopeless—
asking them to do better;
their toxicity has turned
me into hardcore glitter.

And now I shower
all those in my path,
and I fucking sparkle
as I spew my wrath.

They treated me poorly
when I acted like a lady,
and so now I will twinkle
while I go fucking crazy.

This is what they made me.

Oh, I will wear a
crown that shimmers;
as they spew hate,
I will still glimmer.

Though, do not mistake
my dazzling gleam
for a weak damsel
who cannot be mean.

They wanted so badly
to dull my shine,
though, they cannot take
what is truly mine—
this flare that glows
inside my mind.

They tried so hard to
prevent me from glistening,
but my hardcore glitter
keeps on resisting.

So, try if you must,
say what you want,
but hardcore glitter is
sprinkled
all over my
hardcore
heart.

The Witch's Prayer

Give us this day,
our daily rage,
when men will trespass
against us.

We shall not tread lightly
as they prey on and
hunt us daily,
and they give us something
to fight for.

May we seek—and trust—
shelter in our sisters,
with the women
in the gardens
and trees.

May our anger—
and strength—take root
in the forests' floors
as we chant
upon our knees.

May we strengthen
in numbers...
and promiscuity,
as our predators have
always done.

May we drink of
each other,
howl with the wolves,
and cackle
as we run.

May we always
keep them guessing
what's churning in
our minds
as we churn our pots
of stew.

May we bring home
the kindling we'll use
for burning
the herbs and spices
we will brew.

May we give them
the reasons
to call us a witch,
may we drive them
insanely mad.

Please, give us this day,
when all of our rage
is no longer caged
inside of our heads.

Beneath the Wicked Moon

Take me, now,
drink my blood,
lay me softly in
the grass.
Whisper all the
dark secrets
you carry from
your past.
Fill me up with
light from the
wicked moon.
Wrap me up
tightly in all
of your wounds.
Bathe in the noise
of the night sky,
as all of night's
creatures
sing us lullabies.
Drift off to sleep
under this blanket
of stars,
reminisce in the
moments
when the moon
was all ours.

Haunted Hallways

I am lured from my slumber—
a sound in the distance...
awakening from a dream
I wanted to remain in.
Light from the moon
guides me out of my room
and I peek through the curtains...
now, only silence.
Nothing there, as I stare
around this place
with my sullen face.
The fire I put out before bed
is again crackling—an eternal dread.
What did I stir up this time
with all the thoughts in my mind?
Did I call the spirits here
to dance with me in nightly fear?
My demons laugh as I ponder,
and now I'm stuck in the dark to wonder
why I cannot shut them out,
why they're always lingering about...
dragging me around.
There is no peaceful sleep
in this house, where I keep
all my secrets locked inside,
haunting the hallways in my mind.

A Frayed Soul

It was an epic battle amongst the stars,
my soul fighting to win the war.
This combat wasn't new,
I had been here before.
It was my turn for a win—
to gain something more.

But my choices were contested,
and other souls pulled while I resisted.
How much had they invested?
Oh, I felt so conflicted.

I tried to reason
and to bargain,
but this dispute
had gone too far, and

the games they played were unfair—
unscrupulous, even, but they didn't care.
To gain the upper hand, did I dare...
offer a morsel that I could share?

It all felt too much to bear.

Could my soul survive another?
Was I always meant to suffer?
My soul is craving something other
than this torture—this soulful strife;
for far too long, I've been deprived.
I really tried to win this time.

I was supposed to have a different life.

Though, all of the beauty inside of me
wasn't strong enough to keep fighting...

I lost.

My soul was ripped away from me,
now stuck in a life not meant for me;
just wasting time until I can be
returned to contest my eternity.

Until that day,
I will stay...
comforting a soul
that has been frayed.

Midnight Conformity

I do not follow the leader,
nor will I jump off a cliff
behind them;
societal standards
mean nothing to me—
call it an act of defiance.
I will pierce my face
and color my hair,
wear whatever the
fuck I want to wear;
no matter my age,
I do not care
about these made-up
rules.

Though, as the night
is getting near,
and the moon's glow
begins to appear,
I find myself dreaming
of what could be
if I had allowed people
to influence me...

Would I be someone else
entirely?

Oh, the thoughts I have
inspiring me

during my nightly
midnight conformity.

Girly Things

I like girly things
like equal rights
and shiny rings
constructed from the
souls
of my enemies.

I like girly things
like all things pink,
like the color of their
cheeks
when I call them
misogynistic creeps.

I am but a girl,
so I *must* need a
man,
though I like girly things
like bashing them over
the head

when they grab my arm
or they grab my waist,
pull out my girly knife
and leave them bleeding
in the streets.

I like girly things
like abortion rights,
and I like making
grown men cry.

I like girly things
like equal pay
and watching men
lose their minds
when they don't get
their way.

I like girly things
like rainbows after rain
and all the pride
on the passersby
walking in the parade.

I like girly things
like supporting other women,
and making sure they know
when a man is cheating
on them.

I like girly things
like wearing what I want,
fixing up my hair and face,
not knowing where
my fucking place
is

which isn't in the kitchen
or caring for the kids;
my place is in the resistance,
taking down the men.

I Live for the Night

The darkest of moments
bring the darkest ideas,
the darkest words,
the darkest bliss
flowing from my fingertips,
soaking in the darkest shadows,
opening my darkened heart,
painting the darkest meadows
that take me to the darkest forests
covered in the darkest leaves
hiding me from the darkest parts
beneath the darkest trees
until the dark is lighter
and I must come out
craving yet another
dark to come around.

Fancy a Cocktail?

She is sitting there,
legs extended,
one crossed over
the other.

Her red dress is
shining,
blinding,
her skin
so smooth.

She is beauty and sexy;
he's already undressing
her
with his eyes,

salivating over this
stranger
sitting there at the
bar.

If he hurries,
he could get her number
before his wife
arrives.

She looked like you once,
you know?

Is that so?

He knows she is flattered
as she takes out a napkin
and writes a little
note.

While he was in the
bathroom
his wife came asking
the bartender,
where did he go?

And now he has returned
hoping to
score
as she passes his drink.

They taught us this trick
and all—or nothing—
is fair
in love
or war.

So, she buys him a drink
keeping her note a
secret
until he finishes
it.

She stands up to go
and leaves him that note;
upon reading it,
he falls
to the
floor.

Apothecary

Toil and trouble
my cauldron
of bubbles
is spilling
over the top.

They asked
for a cure,
and I said
I'm quite sure
there is no
such a thing
from death.

But they were greedy
and threw me their pennies
and demanded a twisted
curse.

They claimed me a witch,
though I don't mix
my potions with frog sweat
or tears.

I prefer to brew
my rage-filled stew
with the hearts of
my enemies.

So, I took their coins
and asked them to join
as I set the table for
dinner.

Crazed Cats

With their sneaky, quiet
movements,
and their mesmerizing
eyes,
prancing around
with all of their nine
lives;
never a fear...
except when the vacuum
is near—
but that doesn't stop
them
from crying for supper,
screaming like someone
who's been starved
forever;
they do not care
that you're their feeder
of snacks,
they will gladly find
your covered feet and
attack;
dashing and zooming,
climbing walls that are
looming
with shadows dancing,
driving them mad—
but, alas...
they are crazed cats.

Dark Beauties

There are still far too many little girls
being told they should be
pretty, gentle, quiet, and kindly,
cross your legs, smile sweetly...

but I have not forgotten the little girls
who have a darker side they cloak,
hiding in the shadows, trying to cope
until they can grow and part
from all of the standards holding
back their gothic hearts.
Pretty on the outside only
gets you so far;
don't be afraid to show the world
all of your darkest parts.

Dream fearlessly. Dream endlessly. Dream dark.

A Quiet Solace

My solace is quiet;
my solace—my retreat,
away from a world
not meant for me;
my soul aches
for another place
where every woman
has no fear
of ruling men
bringing them
to tears.
I slip away
from all the pain
inside of my nest,
my sweet escape.
I feel rather cozy inside,
for in my solace
I can hide
from a destructive
world outside.
I find comfort
in my chambers
where I can be
fully me,
away from all
the strangers—
my heart safe
from danger.

Where the Soul Goes

Does our soul get a choice—who to be, where to go?
Or is our energy ripped away from the stars—suddenly
when new life is born?
Was I meant for this existence,
or was I meant for more?

I want to believe that my soul has chosen
this path for my earthly bones,
and that there is some purpose here—
some lessons to learn before I return home.

Why would anyone decide
to be thrown into an anxious life,
no escape and nowhere to hide—
yearning for the day my body dies?

I hope my soul knew what it was doing.
Did it choose this life without refusing?
Or is this soul limbo just a dance
to which my limbs haven't yet learned the steps?

I want to believe in eternity,
where my soul no longer needs
to battle and wrestle with anger and angst—
a much, much kinder place...

though, I often wonder
how many times my soul will ponder
a new decision to return
until I have been taught all I need to learn.

Maybe only then
I will no longer carry the burden
of picking and choosing
my own life's torture.

Oh, would all my decisions be different
if I knew without a doubt
that my soul will one day be given
to a place where no one goes without?

I often dream and wish to know...
where, oh where will my soul go
when this planet—this existence—
is no longer my home.

The Storyteller

The seamstress stitches
with her threads,
the quilter with
her patches;
the baker mixes
ingredients,
and the candlemaker
creates with waxes.

A singer blends notes
and chords,
while the band combines
its instruments;
the choir is building
harmonies,
while the healers
patch up the sick.

The painter uses color—
beautiful strokes of art;
and the poet uses words
to break—and heal—hearts.

I am a word weaver,
that is my fate—
my craftsmanship
that I create.

I weave my words
like a web, from
all the endless beauty—
and misery—in my head.

Sometimes my creations are
like stars—bright in the sky,
and then, like lightning
in a storm, they strike.

As I carefully weave
my words,
a story grows—of
pain, of hurt.

But just like in a
fairytale storybook,
my words are weaved
and made to look
like happy endings
can be true;
that's what a storyteller
is born to do.

Misshaped Heart

Many think I care too much
about problems that are not mine,
as if I must be buried in it
for it to be worth my time.

Why do I care—they wonder—
if it doesn't affect me;
though, I cannot comprehend
how they can walk around so blindly.

The sick are getting sicker,
and no medicine can help the poor;
while the rich are getting richer,
shutting us out and locking their doors.

I am not sure how evil grows,
it must be fed from something dead,
and watered with the tears of those dying,
and the evil sprouts while they're lying.

We cannot even ask for help;
they'll send their soldiers—order our death,
if we do not fall in line
and hold our breath
until we suffocate
in our sleep;
how do we stop evil and greed?

I don't know how to make
people care for one another;
I feel alone on my path,
trapped in the dark.

Oh, why is my soul weathered
and torn apart?
I must have a misshaped heart.

Beneath the Roots

There was once beauty all around us,
in the sky, the clouds, the trees.
And then man corrupted all of it;
all that's left is dry, dead leaves.
I search for beauty
through the pollution,
but all I see along the beach is
trash and plastic killing our oceans.
We can't have nice things,
the rich men will steal it,
then they'll call it taxes
and say we owe it,
though our dollars are never recycled
back into our planet.
They take it all and still want more,
a million...a billion...a trillion—
while the rest of us are getting poor.
I'm losing sight of all the light,
the world is looking darker.
As we starve and thirst,
they're filling up their pockets.
I want to see the beauty hidden
behind all of the greed—
a curtain hanging over
the wizard we cannot see.
We ask for better for all people—
all of those in need.
Though, the wizard is evil,
he won't set us free.

Send my bones back to the earth,
oh, Goddess, please—
buried in beauty
beneath the roots of the trees.

Howling at the Moon

Oh, Mother Goddess,
we call to you
from the earth
beneath the moon

We thank you for your light,
your sparkling stars
lighting up the night

You are gracious,
you paved the way
for women to find
their place

amongst the forests,
hidden in the trees,
the only place we
choose to be

We thank you
for your gracious gifts
and we honor your name

In Mother Goddess's name...

awwww-woooo...

howling at the moon.

A Bloody Love Letter

Validation

Why, oh why
do I crave validation,

the desperate need for that affection

bring you to my attention

as I seek love not mentioned.

Give me the words that soothe my soul,
bandage my heart, and keep me whole

for a small bit longer

until I feel stronger

feed me the words of affirmation

please, I beg of you,

just a morsel, of

validation?

Dear Universe,

I am sorry, Universe.

I yelled at you.

I didn't mean to.

Sometimes the weight is heavy,

but I realize

you gift me every day

when you feed me words

straight to the page

through my brain

through my hand.

You are my beautiful Karma.

You Only See the Darkness

I don't care what you think you see
on the surface;
you probably see a little wildness and you think to yourself...
promiscuity;
you think to yourself...
fun.

You can't seem to take a woman seriously
who decorates her body
and doesn't cover up.

I have painted myself
to hide some scars,
to shield myself
from disappointment,
from harm.

You aren't allowed to see
the absolutely overwhelming,
soul shattering
heartbreak
of the little girl
who never got to say goodbye
to her daddy.

You will never have the joy of seeing
the way her eyes race across the pages
of a book that keeps her heart and mind
wanting more...racing.

You cannot experience the tenderness,
the nurturing, and the softness
of her touch...

You only see the toughness, the armor, the shell.
You only see the layers that she has wrapped around herself.
You see the dark, you see the unique.

You see wild, and easy, and fun.
And because of that...
you will never, ever know what she has actually become.

Hi, it's Me, Alt Bar♥bie!

Bar♥bie is Punk.
she picks up her
fucking trash...

she cares for the
animals
she cares for the
kids
she teaches little girls
to say NO to men.

Bar♥bie is Punk.
she's not afraid of
fucking rainbows
she dances right on top
of angry men's toes.

You'll find her in the bleachers
cheering on the women,

"Oh, she's so weird. She like, doesn't
like men!"

Bar♥bie is Punk.
she knows how to coexist
with all the other fucking
weirdos
just like her and her
friends.

Bar♥bie wears pink.
Bar♥bie wears black.
She will also be decked out
in leopard
lacy
flats.

Bar♥bie is cool.
Bar♥bie is punk.
I was raised with *Barbie*
and I give lots of fucks!
♥
P.S. It's like, totally cool to return your shopping carts too, you bastards!
♥
P.S.S. Give the homeless a fucking dollar, assholes!!
♥
Oh, and by the way,
if you're not punk,
you.fucking.SUCK!
♥
Stay punk, kids!

Sincerely,

Alt Bar♥bie

Gothic Heart

She's a song bird in the morning;
she's a wise, old owl at night.

Listen to her tears, my dear,
tell her it's alright
to not be strong endlessly;
it's okay to cry.

The beauty is in the flowers,
a bunk bed for the bees,
sleeping peacefully
amongst the seeds.

And also in the night sky,
bats flying by,
and the wolves in the distance,
howling overhead.

Flames burn brighter
within the dark;
it's okay to have
a gothic heart.

To the Beautiful Souls I Know

Oh, my loves,
we're drowning here
in this raging river,
capsized, waterfall near.

I could never conquer this alone—
on my own—you...you
give me hope

with your beautiful hearts,
and kind, loving souls—
how you pour into...
everyone...
but you.

Please, love yourself harder,
deeper, purer...
see yourself as I see you,
notice all the beauty in my mirror,

how your eyes glisten when
you speak of things you love,
how your smile widens
and your face lights up
when happiness shines down on you,
you beautiful, fucking soul.

Now, grab this rope.

I can't do this alone.

Mad Girl, Bad Girl

First, you become a sad
girl
Then, you become a mad
girl
Next, you become a bad
girl
And he'll wish he never lied,
girl.

Yes, he had a choice
and he let you down;
walk away, girl,
this shit's over now.

Have a decent cry,
girl
Then go dry your eyes,
girl
There are so many better guys,
girl;
Pick up your fucking crown.

If revenge is what you want,
girl
Then I'll be by your side,
girl;
But blocking that shit
is how you heal your pride,
girl.

Book of Spells

It's all a bunch of hocus pocus...
enchantments and potions

and elixirs,
a conjuration of the proper ingredients,

herbologist, I insist

pre-heat the cauldron...or an oven

chop the herbs and steep the honey, fresh
from the bees outside

melt the maple syrup into the brandy,
just a small bit will do

toil and trouble, my cauldron of bubbles,
set to boil over the top

but just you wait, the secret ingredient will be
added just before, don't stop

stirring and mixing, do not let it brew

I know what I'm doing, I promise I do

or perhaps that's just...the mushrooms

Magical Library

Dear Goddess of the Universe,

I do not ask for money or fame. I do not ask
for sun over rain. I do not ask for blue skies
every day. I do not wish for tempting good looks.

I simply ask for books.

A secret library hidden everywhere I look. Close
my eyes and step inside, and bathe in all the words.

Get lost in the pages, filling up my mind, and cradling
my heart when my favorite character dies.

Though, I do not ask for a Prince Charming, I saved
myself long ago, I do wish for more happy ever afters
for the kindest of souls.

Send a Robin Hood to feed the poor and deliver
poisonous apples to every villain's door.

I wish for a forever escape that I can turn to on the
darker days, take me to another place where I choose
when the bookmark is placed.

A reprieve from the hate. Just a few more pages...
one more chapter...a magical library ever after.

Little Black Love Bird

Just because my heart is a bit dark
does not mean it doesn't pump blood
and love into the world

even blood can be black

and even though I speak loudly and
scream passionately does not mean
I'm not screaming out of love

my heart was red once upon a time,
a bright, glowing, apple red...perfect
with caramel sauce

though it has grown along with my bones
and it has transitioned into something
different...dark red...crimson

and I'm not sure if it is still bathing there or
if it is metamorphosing into something...darker...
shades of brown...or charcoal grey

but it still beats and it still loves and it still misses
and it still adores and it still cries with compassion
for other beating souls, especially the...different ones

even souls are choosing parties, if you quiet your mind...

...you can *feel* the good ones

oh, I'm just a little love bird in a vulture's mind, twisted
and turned all of the time

even the Beast had a happy ending

I still hope for a fairytale ending...even if it means
my soul finds love after death

only then will my little black love bird heart get to rest

A Heart of Glass

Maybe I should have chosen the glass slippers
over the glass heart

maybe then I would be standing on top of the world
shattering ceilings, raining shards

but alas, I chose a heart of glass

and now it shatters on a daily basis, I'm not sure how
it keeps mending, I accidentally cut myself often...
forgetting it is sharp

I suppose there is a glass mender just like a tooth fairy,
picking up the fallen out pieces while making room for
new glass to be installed

it takes a few business days to arrive, they must be in
short supply

the world is shattering too many hearts, all the broken
parts are polluting our landfills

and our oceans

and starving our children

and stealing medicine from the sick

and murdering. so much murdering

shattered

glass shattering, my soul must be made of glass, too;
what's a girl to do...

I should have chosen the fucking shoe

This Girl is on Fire

I don't know how she fucking does it, like a fucking
magic trick. Every time she stumbles, she fucking
stands again.

She kept hitting goals, thinking that was success, but
she never really knew best, and so she messed up
again and again.

Though, she never did quite win a lot of battles, she
has won a few, and she is still going; she refuses to quit.
Again and again.

Goddess damn it is hot in here.

Her body burns like a furnace because she is the fuel
to the ignition, a flame burning with intention, no need
for a lighter,

this girl is on fire!

You Shall Live on Forever in My Words

Don't worry, I never forget about you. You'll always be
there, that comforting dark cloud in my mind. A storm
I'm not sure if I need to run from or face. Every day is
different.

I'm turning forty soon...that's how old you were when...
you know. Just three weeks after that big 4-0...you were
here no more. Just taken.

I truly thought you were faking, like that time you hid from
us kids all damn night long...where the fuck were you
hiding? I'll make you tell me one day.

And so I am approaching that age.

And things are clearer now. I didn't know much back
then...just a twelve-year-old kid. I was pissed.
How fucking dare you!

I understand now. I understand a little more at least.
And maybe one day you will tell me your story, and we
can rewind the happy times, replay on repeat. Please
skip episode nine. That was a rough time.

And a lot of the times before then; there weren't too many
of the good ones early on, remember? I don't remember
much, but I do remember your love.

Tough, rough, hard, dark love. That must be where I got it
from. I can't believe you gave this to me, what did I do to
hurt you?

Never mind. I know. It wasn't completely your fault. I'm
still lost...turning forty. I suppose you were, too.

Anyway, I still miss you. Even though I'll soon be older than you...maybe anyway.

Oh, and I did make some of my dreams come true, but maybe you heard.

Well, gotta go. I'll see you next time, when I write you into my words.

Writing My Eulogy

Dear loved ones,
it is time
for me to say
goodbye.
Do not cry,
please, dry your
eyes.
Though my time
is over here
on this planet
we call earth,
my soul was always
meant for more;
I've known this
since birth.
There is beauty
in the stars
at night—
the flaming fire
burning bright,
and there is comfort
in the moon—
quite a wonderful
sight.
My soul will know
where to go,
the Universe calls
to me;
this life isn't meant
to last forever—
this existence is
not our eternity.

The Christians
may say
my sinning soul
will be sent
straight to hell,
and if that's so,
I'll dance with
the devil,
once I arrive
down there.
My soul was born
of fire—
the Aries always
are.
If you begin
to miss me,
look for me
in the stars.

Dead Inside

Though my black heart is filled with love, it is also
filled with dark.

I cannot help that the furnace was higher, burning
brighter, the day that I was born.

Melted tar spilling on my pure heart. Polluted, I'm sure.

And as small pieces of my heart were chiseled away
in this life, tar seeping through the cracks...turning
my blood black.

I always preferred the glow of the stars in the dark.
My favorite part.

I can't ever seem to get it right, and so I stopped trying...
a while ago.

It's not that I'm now trying to hide, I'm just more myself
on my own, in my home, alone. Day or night.

Maybe I'm just dead inside...

Moth to a Flame

I once envisioned myself a firefly...wandering aimlessly,
lighting up the night, brightening the sky, just by being me

I tried to bring peace, I really did, but peace did not accept
my invitation for tea

I offered peace a bribe but it was declined

I am not sure what my soul did in its previous earthly life to
deserve this fire that is burning inside, did I ask for this?

maybe I did

maybe I was meant to live this life with rage

no longer leaving it caged

feral

I was born in the fire, and maybe that is why my phoenix
soul never lets go, it keeps rising, returning, yearning...
for something

like a horcrux, I'm just chasing it around the universe
looking for a piece, not knowing how many are left to find

in due time

I suppose I can manage one more round if I must, though I
need rest, I can always take a nap

and then I will rise again from my soul's slumber party and
now my firefly light has burned out, just exhaustion and
doubt

and I see it burning, all of it, and I am not afraid

I am running toward it ferociously

like a moth to a flame

Spellbound

Mesmerized
inside those eyes
of deep green
and gold;
I am sold,
please, let me hold
on to you
a little while
longer.
What is this
hold you've put
on me;
am I even participating
willingly?
Why can I
not find
another sight
to set my eyes
upon?
Why is this fire
burning inside
me, when you are
all wrong for me?
You lead me
away, without a
sound...how?
It must be a curse,
a trick, a
spell...bound.

Gothic Love

I know it might sound a bit creepy,
but my soul wants to slip out and slide into your heart and
cuddle while it's beating

riding the spinning tea cups at the amusement park,
screaming "again!"

then maybe a little afternoon nap stuck inside your chest,
she could climb the tower to the tip top (her favorite part)
and read a while

she sure does love to read, and to read *you* would be...
icing on the cake,

oh, it is time for us to move, ate too much and feeling
sleepy, she will slide down into your toes and have you
leaping

oh, to frolic again and bathe in the dandelions, make a
wish

if she wasn't so exhausted, she would climb back to the
top of the beanstalk and get lost in your library

but she is weary

please wrap her in your hands so gently, hold her softly,
and tuck her back into your heart bed, slumber party

she is yours now

please, take care of her

I gothically love you

for bloody eternity

My Bloody Eternity

Dearly Departed,

We are gathered here on this full moon night
at the gravesite

to express our excitement for your arrival

and my condolences for your wicked soul

it must be strange, us meeting here like this, but I have
always been connected to your soul...it's like we're old
soulmates

I cannot be certain if I knew you in an earthly life before...
the soul forgets such trivial things such as...breathing...
life

but I am certain, wickedly positive that our frayed souls
have been tethered together for some time, keeping the
other from ripping at the seams

and so, it seems...I was sent here to this very grave at this
very time...for you

welcome home, gothic goddess

may your dark soul forever know gothic love in your bloody
eternity...your wicked forever after

Yours wickedly,
Gothic Love

My Gothic Valentine

Oh, to be seen...my soul finally acknowledged,
appreciated, validated.

I always knew it was meant for more, I just wasn't
sure how long it would take.

I had nothing to do but wait.

And so, I wrote poetry about you, knowing one day
I'd be able to read it to you...still wondering what your
eyes looked like...in your previous life.

But my soul knows your soul, and we were meant to be
here, on this wicked night, beneath the wicked moon.
Swoon.

Though we do not need coffins for our earthly bodies,
they will return to the fire where we were transpired.

My mind had to walk the path of death on its own,
no longer home to my soul...my heart followed me,
of course; she was always on my side.

But that *damn* mind.

It's about time she gets a break. She's the reason we all
ached. And why you and I never met until now.

On this night, such a delight,
to finally dine with my
gothic valentine.

Happily Ever After Death

Dearly beloved,

We are gathered here tonight, under the moon light, in this forest tucked inside the trees

to honor the gothic souls—fog on the breeze.

On cloudy days, our souls come out to play, seeking comfort in the haze.

We are now joined in unholy union beneath the wicked moon

and

we can finally rest in peace

a comfortable ease

a final breath

happily ever

after death.

A Bloody Love Letter

Dear You,

(you know who you are)

I'm writing you this bloody fucking love letter because I bloody fucking love you.

I love your wicked heart and your witchy soul. You are fucking beautiful when you smile...and when you laugh, and when you cry, and when you fight. So. Fucking. Beautiful.

I know life sucks a lot of days. Some days your head is barely above water. And you do not deserve that shit! You just keep proving you are the fucking strongest, most powerful person. You hold all that fucking power!

Don't you ever fucking forget how much you shine...the dark parts, too. (Secret: the dark is my favorite.)

Signed with all my darkest love from the bottom of my wicked heart,

Another Badass Beautiful Woman ♡

Amanda L. Ball

Wicked Dreams, Goodnight

An Ode to Poe

I walk alone in the cemetery
at night when the moon
is brightest,
for I want to have light
to sit by your grave
and read you poetry
in the silence.

I read to you of the
unkindness
of the ravens approaching,
though I told them, *no more.*

And of the murder of crows
who stole...my heart for...
evermore.

And on the gates, I heard
them,
tapping,
tapping as I was reading...
warning me of something?
Though, I cannot be sure.

They may be crazed when the
full moon is on display...
yet, I *still* cannot be sure.

And so I read you Edgar,
and Hemingway, and Plath...
I would never leave out Maya
who keeps us all rising when
days are black.

And for this reason, I prefer
the night, the moon, the
stars;
a poetic picnic
in this poetic graveyard

stretched out my legs
over your grave
feeling the soil between
my toes

wishing—or witching—
for darkness
and nothing more.

Amanda L. Ball

Echoes of a Haunted Past

Memories are always fleeting,
the mind deciding
which pieces to share and
which to keep in hiding.

Flipping through the catalogue
inside of my mind,
desperately searching and
hoping to find

a beautiful photograph
from a happier time,
but so many are blurry or
undeveloped—a terrible crime.

My mind has blocked them
deep inside,
lost in the pages, I play
seek while they hide.

Darker memories in the forefront,
concealing those in the back;
I need a trick of the mind to
drown out the echoes of a haunted past.

But my mind is unconcerned
with my weeping soul,
drowning out the tears,
and I'm losing control.

I've been here before—
dancing this dance,
begging my mind
for an advance.

Please, move on,
let it all go...

Though the echoes of
my haunted past
are all that I know.

Where My Skull is Buried

Let me lie in peace, here
in the dark
surrounded by my art...

the melodies in my head,
the stories I have shed
onto the pages, poured
from my soul.

Cover me up in thorny brambles...
my heart in shambles,
searching for another taste
as my insides ache.

Release my soul from the hold
my mind has a tightly woven
grasp on...my heart battling,
punctured, wounded

searching for home...

so lost, not knowing where I belong,
asking to be carried...

and my soul laid to rest
where my skull is buried.

Where Have All the Lovers Gone?

We've been turned into rebels
because we refuse to back down,
we refuse to give in to their
hate and their greed.

We've been ridiculed,
forgotten, exiled,
left to die in the street.

And so we had no choice
but to take up arms,
to fight, to resist;
no one safe from harm.

I yearn to go back to
a place in the stars,
where hatred is evicted;
though it seems so far

away from where
we are today—
a billion galaxies
and light years away.

Maybe they're all floating
nearby in another dimension,
or inside a spaceship
we avoid with apprehension.

It is getting so dark
in this place that we live;
I wasn't meant to fight;
I was meant to give.

It seems so hopeless
when you have a lover's heart,
but you're stuck in turmoil
in the dark.

If only I could just escape
into the realm
outside of hate
and bask in the place
where all the lovers
have gone to wait.

When Witches Dream

Stories say witches dream
of love spells and potions,
and turning men into toads,
or eating children for lunches

making black cats speak...
and do their bidding in the
streets,
poking dolls with pins
and cackling as they scream.

The stories tell of a long,
crooked nose,
of hexes, and curses, of
sleeping
with bones

but these stories are told
by scared, insecure men
who know that witches
aren't afraid of them.

So, let me tell you the truth
of it all—
when witches dream,
they don't dream of
witchcraft at all...

they dream of flying into the
sunset,
dashing through the sky
with all of their witchy
friends
as the bats fly by

dancing under a
sparkling moon,
loving one another,
and Mother Nature, too.

Witches dream of peace on
earth,
coexisting with all of the
creatures,
protecting the land,
holding each other's hands,
living harmoniously together.

Though, witches do love to
dream
of cursing evil men while
they sleep,
witches wish and dream for
better
than all the poor people have
been given.

Witches dream of smudging
away
all of the evil that is in play
and bringing more good into
the world...
that is truly what witches are
for.

Magic Mushroom

Magic mushroom in the ground,
I am lost, hoping to be found.
Please tell me if I am bound
to forever wander anxiously around.

Magic mushroom on earth's floor,
can you grow me into something more—
into a creature that is adored;
what is this human life even for?

Magic mushrooms, such a treat,
devouring you for some release;
I am only seeking peace—
here inside the forest's trees.

I do not mean to sound so needy,
I only hope to find a remedy
for all the sick, the poor, the greedy;
I wish to sign a peaceful treaty.

Magic mushroom, can you help us?
All of the people are feeling hopeless,
and I do not have enough
magic inside me to soothe the restless.

Oh, Magic Mushroom in the dirt,
is there any hope for earth?
Are our souls even worth
the magic you hold for our rebirth?

Eternal Cloak of Haze

I prefer to walk in the fog,
the haze
where I can be shadowed,
left unscathed
by all the prying eyes
trying to see deep inside
all the secrets that I hide

Deep in the fog, the haze,
I'm stripped of my insecurities,
and I don't have to place
all of the burdens of the world on me

Like a cloak of invisibility,
the haze wraps around,
protecting me

And the world can just let me be,
leaning on the edge of existing...
resisting...the fall

into my ever after eternity

My Dreams, a Prison

I am a prisoner here—
shackled and chained,
inside my mind, as I
sleep and I dream.

I'm battling beasts and
monsters galore,
I'm begging for mercy
and craving more.

War is raging within my dreams,
I'm being hunted, frightened...
what did I do to deserve this?

How do I take back control
when my mind is dreaming
and taking a toll
on my thoughts
and on my heart?

I'm a prisoner here, in the dark.

Hush Little Asshole

Hush little asshole
don't say a word,
I'm getting tired of
having to flip the bird

Shut your mouth
don't tell me to smile,
or I'll have to say
something extra vile

Stop staring at me
like a creep,
before I have to knock you
off your feet

Hush little asshole,
walk on by,
don't touch me, or
you'll have to die.

Night, night!

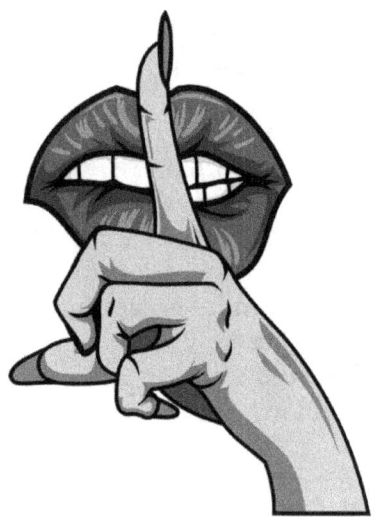

Candy Castles

I was made to believe
in all things pink
and glittery unicorns,
strawberry hair,
bears that care,
and bright rainbows
on which I could sleep.

I learned not to eat the apples
or touch the spinning wheel,
to not let down my hair
when others were near,
and not to wear
glass shoes.

They wanted me to trust
the white knights
and beg them to be saved.

But I learned to tame the
dragons
that kept getting in my way.

I could build a candy castle,
luring the young with treats
as they fall into my cauldron
and I prepare a feast.

I was made to believe
that the dark, angry women
were the witches we should
avoid

and princesses are just the
princes' toys.

Though through the mirror
on the wall,
I learned who was the wisest
of them all.

And I stirred my potions
in time for the solstice
and enjoyed my candy corn...

brewing in my tower,
holding the power,
knights locked in the
dungeon
beneath my floor.

Black Rabbits

White, like snow,
their fur, it glows
and everyone wants
a look
as they hop through
the prairie,
so very fast
and cute.

The black rabbits
stay hidden,
as they are called
omens
that no one wants
to impart,
so they remain
underground
until the moon
is out;
they're freer in
the dark.

They find one another
under the moon,
where they feast
and they sing
and they love.
And as the sun rises
and daylight approaches,
they choose to cover
back up,
remaining in the shadows...
hoping the night
will come again
soon enough.

Death at the Door

I stare out my window
into my garden, bare;
I daydream of a fuller time
when more flowers were
growing there.

I dreamed of a secret door,
behind the thorny bush;
only I knew of its existence,
slide in the key...turn...push.

Enter a world
where there are
no thorns,
and women
are held to the
highest regard...

take a nap
beside the tree,
not worried man
will bother me.

I slept too long,
the sun is setting;
I must hurry on my way
and get back home
by the light of the moon
hoping I can return again
someday.

I get to the door...
it locked behind me,
I cannot find the key!

Panic sets in...but then,
I wonder...

is this what it means to die in
peace?

Reincarnation

I am not afraid of death,
nor am I afraid of mistakes
or regrets.

I have lived my earthly life
the way that I want
despite all the strife.

Though, I do believe my soul
was made for more
than this.

Battling pain constantly—
in my mind and
in my body.

Watching people—
children—
starve to death;
why is greed not forbidden?

I have to turn off the news—
the reports of endless
suffering and abuse.

My soul craves something
more;
surely there must be
better in store.

My bones are weakening
as the abhorrent hate
is strengthening.

There is so much filth
covering our land,
oil being spilled.

This isn't what I signed up
for;
oh, please, let there be
something more.

My heart is utterly famished,
craving a different
planet.

Maybe my soul can return
as a star once this life
has adjourned.

196

Vampiress

She bathes in Merlot...
at least I think so;
her hair bright red
like cherries on her head.

Her lips of raspberries—
tempting, but no...
I think she bites;
or maybe I hope so.

I watch her walk
and hear her talk
and I am transfixed...
is this a trick?

I have never felt fluttering
feelings like this,
as I watch her sip,
licking the wine from her lips.

The lady of the night,
they say, but who am I
to judge her ways?

She is captivating,
luring me in with her eyes...
are those fangs?

Indeed.

Well-played, Vampiress,
in your black, velvet dress;
I confess...
I knew it all along.

Soul Searching

Under the dirt,
my toes buried
into the earth,
I belong here—
under the moon,
my youth gone
too soon.
And now I must
pay the tolls
to all the trolls
while the goblins
steal my lunch.
The kings in their
towers
looking right down
here,
always laughing
at us.
I would rather return
to the forest
with the wolves,
so uncertain
if I should belong
in their pack.
Looking for where
I fit in
before this life
is through.
Searching for answers...
after my bones are buried,
will my soul know
what to do?

The Writer's Prayer

I cross my heart
and hope to thrive;
otherwise,
what's the point
in being alive?

There must be
some meaning here—
much greater than
eternal fear.

It is not a fiery
hell I dread,
it's all the what-ifs
inside my head.

It is not a god
I fear or loathe,
it's all the claims
of certainty told.

My mind more deep
than they know;
I'm not choosing a faith
to torture my soul.

I am choosing
my own path,
believing in things
much more vast

than a god of fury,
a god of control;
I've never been good
at doing what I'm told.

So, if I shall die
before I wake,
please, allow the witches
my soul to take;

they will need it
more than I,
as the energy
of my mind

is carried to
the place
where dreamers and
writers go to embrace.

Her Fairytale Ending

Do not call me a princess,
as I follow no leader.
Though, I'm always a
student,
I'm also a teacher.
A goddess, protective
of all of her flock;
a warrior, a weapon,
taking note of her stock.
I am no queen—
no one shall bow;
we will be equals,
partners in battle.
I'll suit up my armor,
not hide in my tower;
I don't need to be saved
by rich fucking cowards.
I will ride in
on my own steed;
I don't need a knight
rescuing me.
No, I'm not a princess,
and I don't need a prince;
I'll choose the bear
in the forest with friends.

Night's Light

The moon knows my secrets
and has felt my sadness,
she has dried my tears
and redirected my madness.

She has been there, waiting,
for me in silence
when I toss and turn,
my mind teetering, unbalanced.

She watches patiently
as I beg for sleep,
hugging me gently
when I weep.

She knows I need her
most at night
and she's always there,
my own night light.

Dream Weaver

Sewn into the pockets
of all of the children,
tiny, buttoned patches
tucked away, hidden.

Like the tooth fairy,
she only comes at night,
slips in through the window
to give you a fright.

She quilts all the stories
there in their minds
as they slumber restlessly
throughout the night.

Sometimes she is gentle
when her heart isn't weeping,
and in those rare moments
she makes you smile while
you're
sleeping.

But most of her patterns
require something dark,
a morsel of her soul
left inside your heart.

And you imagine
all your worst fears
and you carry them with you
for too many years.

For she has threaded
all of your angst,
your worries, insecurities,
all the dark things you think

right inside
the pocket of your mind,
buried deep...
your soul for her to keep.

Zodiac

At my core, I am the sun—
the role I play in this world,
my life's motivations.

When alone in the night,
the moon knows my heart—
all of the emotions I hide inside.

Though when I ascend—when I rise—
the people see who I am
when I carry around my disguise.

Oh, my Aries Sun rages with passion;
my Pisces Moon shows much compassion;
my Virgo Rising craves utter perfection.

My quick-witted Aries Mercury rules with honesty,
though my Aries Venus is adventurous and fiery;
my Mars in Taurus leaves me determined...and stubborn.

I was born with Jupiter in Aquarius, forced into
a life of progressive humanitarianism...oh, no wonder
I'm a mess.

Birthed with Uranus in Sagittarius, I rebel from all religion;
my free-spirited and forward thinking prefers I pray to
Mother Nature, or the Goddess Universe—
energy all around us.

Born of my generation, with Capricorn in Neptune,
in my fourth house I have doubts, of a traditional
family setting.

And all of my Zodiac parts
pull and tug my Scorpio's Pluto heart
filled with fearless, mysterious magnets
healing me when I'm in the dark.

Though, I'm still not done, a Scorpio in Saturn
leaves me resilient, strong, and growing.
It takes this bundled mess from the stars
and guides me always towards regeneration.

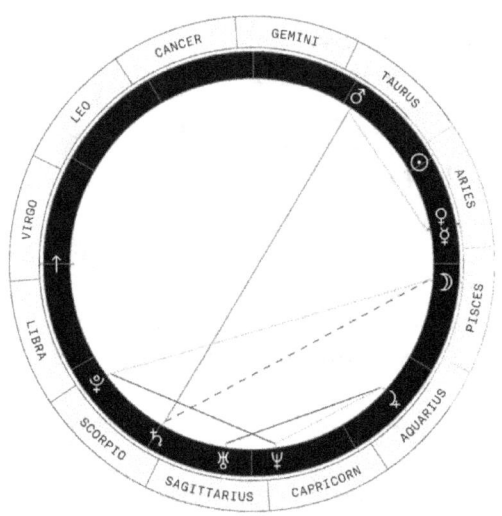

A Grim(m) Poet

I was once the romantic poet,
love scenes filling my heart;
believing in happy ever afters,
finding beauty in all of the scars.

But now this space my mind
is filling up inside my head
is darker, creepier, witchier...
a world filled with revenge and dread.

Weaving the stories
of vengeful witches,
of angry women
scaring the devil,
of snakes for hair,
and graves gone bare
as we dance with all
of the corpses.

Though, Shel is still inside my ink,
and Seuss gives me my rhymes,
I now bathe in Grimm
in the dark, inside my mind.

Blanket Fort of Stars

The coven is calling,
howling my name;
to the forest
I shall return.
We will dream and rest
in the daytime
and gather in the night,
make friends with
the vampires and werewolves
underneath the moon's light.
We'll share our stories,
and dance naked
under the stars,
protected by the
forest's trees—
nature filling up
our hearts.
We can make our beds
here on earth's floor,
in our blanket fort of stars,
while the fireflies
light up the sky
and the fairies sing
us lullabies
goodnight.

Wicked Dreams, Goodnight

The day is done and
night has come,
my favorite time, by far;
when I can hide away
with all my secrets
and my demons,
when they come out
to play.

The moon is bright
behind the haze,
still lighting up the snow;
as my mind drifts
in a daze...
time to tuck in my bones.

Crawl in bed to read
a ghostly tale of woe,
but my mind has other plans
of writing poetry
to my soul.

And so I linger in between
my thoughts and my slumber,
waiting for the witch's call
to tell me the day is over.

So, I tell the moon I love her,
and tuck myself up tight,
wish on the stars, and sing
lullabies until I have
wicked dreams...goodnight.

Sometimes I am political; sometimes I am poetic; sometimes I am silly or sarcastic; all the time, I am passionate.

May we love each other more deeply, hold each other more tightly, and lift each other higher in the darkest of days.

May all your dreams be wickedly sweet.

♡

Epiloque

It was my lifelong dream to publish my own poetry book—as a little girl curled up on her bed writing away. After (finally) publishing my debut poetry book, something sparked in me. I felt our country—our world—was in turmoil. People are begging for help all over the world as they are being tortured and dying unnecessarily. My empathic heart is always overloaded in this world. The best way for me to get out all of that angst, that pain, and anger is to write about it. And so, I wrote all of these poems in this second poetry storybook in only a few weeks' time (yes, really). I attempt to weave my poetry into stories that we can all relate to. Though there is darkness all around us, and sometimes my words are dark, I hope they can still bring some light to this world—some hope and some vengeance in a way. I want to cut open all of the hate, leaving it exposed and seeping out for us all to see clearly. Only then can we bury it. I also hope each of you can not only bury your pain but heal from it and move forward knowing that true wickedness may always exist...but it can also always be defeated.

To all the dark souls out there, you're all beautiful and worthy. We can be a bit dark and still stand strongly in the light. I hope you never have to hide who you truly are.

And never stop enjoying—or reaching for—your wicked dreams.

♡ Amanda

A.K.A. Alt Bar♥bie

Wicked Dreams Goodnight

Bonus Ending

Beauty Became the Beast

There's a fucking beast in me.

She chose the bear,
tamed the bear,
trained the bear,
became the bear.

They want a man-hater, then I'll become their villain,
and that means I will need some victims.

I will need to stock up for winter hibernation,
I can kill and eat at least a few men.

Of course women choose the bear, we have learned how
to tame dragons, and all of the demons they've been
dragging behind them.

There has to be a villain in every story—someone they can
hide behind while the jury is judging.

And so, I will be the beast they lure, though I've been
planning plenty of surprises.

There's a fucking beast in me, and I'm no longer willing to
fight it.

Wicked Dreams Goodnight

Moon Child

(final bonus ending)

Goodnight to all the owls outside, hooting through
the night, posting guard in the trees, hiding out of sight.

Goodnight to all the flying bats, escaping from their caves,
finally getting their turn to start another day.

Goodnight to the vultures feasting on the creatures whose
time has come, continuing the cycle of life, preying from above.

Goodnight to the sun who always goes to bed too soon,
she was never a moon child like me, having a sleepover
with the moon.

Goodnight to the animals who love me endlessly and
comfort my aching heart, they give me purpose and
companionship of which no human has ever been able
to impart.

Goodnight to the wicked souls and the darkest hearts
of wild.

Goodnight to them, goodnight to you.

Goodnight, Moon Child.

The End (for now).

About the Author

Amanda L. Ball has been writing poetry since she was a young girl, having her first poem published in a book for young poets at age 11. It has been her lifelong dream to publish her own collection of poetry, and she made that dream come true before turning 40. She is a loud, relentless voice for social justice and cares deeply about child and animal welfare. *Wicked Dreams Goodnight* is her second published poetry book.

Though she grew up and lived in Texas for 35 years, she has spent time traveling the world, living as a nomad across the country, and currently resides in the state of Maryland with her dog and two cats, enjoying her passion for books and writing.

And she has never, ever stopped dreaming.

Other Works by this Author:

Storm of Enchanted Dreams: a poetic fairytale

www.ingramcontent.com/pod-product-compliance
Lightning Source LLC
Chambersburg PA
CBHW060925120626
46557CB00003B/878